21 July 2007

To Ted —

In honor of LFP

Fred

John

"Onward and Upward"[*]

The Career Trajectory and Memories
of Leonard F. Peltier, M.D., Ph.D.

"A cripple is an individual that is lame or otherwise disabled as a result of injury, disease, or a condition existing since birth. It is an old term of northern European origin and has been used in this sense for over a thousand years; it is a term that is well established in the medical, social, and legal terminology. In the last twenty years, however, cripple has assumed a pejorative connotation and for this reason is disappearing from common usage."

— LEONARD F. PELTIER, 1993
ORTHOPEDICS: A HISTORY AND ICONOGRAPHY
INTRODUCTION, P. XXV.

The small reproductions of "cripples" included throughout this book are reprinted with permission from Peltier, LF, Orthopedics: A History and Iconography. San Francisco: Norman Publishing, 1993 (frontispiece); originally from A Procession of Cripples by Hieronymous Bosch. Die Medizin in der klassischen Malerei, 1903.

"Onward and Upward"*
The Career Trajectory and Memories
of Leonard F. Peltier, M.D., Ph.D.

Janolyn G. Lo Vecchio
Frederick W. Reckling
JoAnn B. Reckling

Foreword by Robert G. Volz

Published by the Clendening History of Medicine Library and Museum
University of Kansas Medical Center
Kansas City, Kansas

*A favorite expression of Leonard's to encourage residents, staff, family and friends...paraphrasing James Russell Lowell: "They must upward still, and onward, who would keep abreast of Truth." From the poem "The Present Crisis," by James Russell Lowell (1844).

Published by the Clendening History of Medicine Library and Museum
University of Kansas Medical Center
Kansas City, Kansas 66160
© 2004 by the Clendening History of Medicine Library and Museum
First Printing
All Rights Reserved, Published 2004
Printed in the United States of America

Library of Congress catalogue card number 2004102622
ISBN 0-9749283-0-5

Contents

∾

Illustrations

༉

Foreword

∾

Reflections on a Four-Decade Association
with Leonard F. Peltier, M.D., Ph.D.

The Kansas Years

My first meeting with Dr. Peltier took place as I was interviewing
as a resident applicant at a number of university orthopedic training
programs in the fall of 1960. This meeting remains as a vivid memory
to this day. To a great measure, this is so because we soon discovered
we had both been raised in Lincoln, Nebraska, attended the same junior
and senior high schools and the University of Nebraska as
undergraduates. I can recall leaving Kansas City after that visit with the
decision to place the University of Kansas Medical Center (KUMC)
training program as my number one choice, ahead of Michigan, Iowa,
Oklahoma and Colorado. Several weeks later, the mail brought an offer
from Dr. Peltier for me to begin as a resident on 1 July 1961. It would
prove to be an opportunity that would dramatically shape my life's
professional career.

The three years I spent under his watchful and critical eye as a
resident were probably the most exciting intellectual learning years of
my career. It was my impression, very soon on, that Dr. Peltier was the
most widely read and scholarly academician I had yet to encounter.
Fluent in German and French, his scientific references were beyond
the grasp of most. At the time of my training at KUMC from 1961 to
1964, the Center was a widely respected regional referral center, one
staffed with nationally known and respected professors who had
developed their own successful specialized practices. Nearly all had

Foreword

∾

Reflections on a Four-Decade Association with Leonard F. Peltier, M.D., Ph.D.

The Kansas Years

My first meeting with Dr. Peltier took place as I was interviewing as a resident applicant at a number of university orthopedic training programs in the fall of 1960. This meeting remains as a vivid memory to this day. To a great measure, this is so because we soon discovered we had both been raised in Lincoln, Nebraska, attended the same junior and senior high schools and the University of Nebraska as undergraduates. I can recall leaving Kansas City after that visit with the decision to place the University of Kansas Medical Center (KUMC) training program as my number one choice, ahead of Michigan, Iowa, Oklahoma and Colorado. Several weeks later, the mail brought an offer from Dr. Peltier for me to begin as a resident on 1 July 1961. It would prove to be an opportunity that would dramatically shape my life's professional career.

The three years I spent under his watchful and critical eye as a resident were probably the most exciting intellectual learning years of my career. It was my impression, very soon on, that Dr. Peltier was the most widely read and scholarly academician I had yet to encounter. Fluent in German and French, his scientific references were beyond the grasp of most. At the time of my training at KUMC from 1961 to 1964, the Center was a widely respected regional referral center, one staffed with nationally known and respected professors who had developed their own successful specialized practices. Nearly all had

served in WWII or the Korean War and thus brought to the Center a formal and highly disciplined professional demeanor that at times could be very intimidating. The times were pre-Medicare, and thus patients were either classified as "private pay" to be generally cared for by the faculty, or patients under a state-assisted financial program, with the latter group generally becoming the responsibility of the resident staff. It was a time when hospital wards were still accepted by the public, and the residents cared for patients who occupied crowded four- and five-bed rooms.

The demands placed upon the orthopedic resident staff were decidedly different than those of today's trainees. For instance, we were responsible for drawing all blood specimens, starting blood transfusions, placing patients in all forms of traction, day and night, scheduling staff and resident surgeries within a rigid time deadline, and of course running our own medically-indigent outpatient clinics. The hours were long. In fact, when my five-year-old daughter once was asked by an adult friend, "What does your Daddy do?" her response was "He never comes home." Our pay was below the poverty level, beginning at $3000 per year as a junior house officer and rising to $3600 as a senior officer. All house officers were directed to wear hospital-issued white pants and shirts made by the state's prison inmates. A $50 per month meal punch card was also provided. It allowed wives and children to join Dad for an inexpensive dinner in the hospital cafeteria when he was on call.

The treatment of fractures was decidedly different in those days, with the emphasis placed on closed treatment. Exceptions of course were hip fractures, in which the fractured femoral head was either secured by pinning or replaced with an Austin-Moore endoprosthesis. Depending upon the pattern of femoral shaft fractures, some were treated with Kuntscher nails, or if comminuted, by a distally-placed skeletal traction pin combined with a Thomas ring. The latter patients were hospitalized until X-ray evidence of some callus about the fracture site was observed. Then they were placed in a half-body spica cast. The issue of hospital time was not a deterrent to care. All tibial fractures were treated closed, and they often required several attempts at cast-wedging to allow for an acceptable degree of alignment. Shortening was usually unavoidable. Fractures of the upper extremity were generally treated with casts; a humeral shaft with a hanging cast; a both-bones of the forearm fracture immobilized in plaster in the correct rotational position. Obviously this approach to fracture care predated the Swiss contribution to internal fixation used today for nearly all types of open and closed fractures. The closed treatment method demanded the skillful application of casts, and all resident-treated cases were reviewed at the Saturday X-ray conference and carefully scrutinized by resident peers and faculty.

KUMC was one of two hospitals running a busy regional emergency center in the Kansas City metropolitan area. Thus, multiply-injured patients were often transported by ambulance from considerable distances. Level I trauma centers with helicopter support were not yet in place. Residents were frequently left to reduce upper extremity fractures without the aid of a general anesthetic. Out of necessity, many of us quickly learned a technique of providing regional anesthesia, specifically axillary blocks.

During my three years as a resident, I was also privy to the compelling research Dr. Peltier was pursuing on the subject of fat embolism, a clinical entity that sometimes occurs following an acute fracture of a major long bone. At that time fat embolism was thought to be of little clinical consequence. In fact, a Massachusetts General Hospital staff orthopedic surgeon of national recognition had written in the late 1950s in a current orthopedic text that he believed the condition did not exist. How wrong this opinion proved to be, and today, in great part due to Dr. Peltier's carefully documented laboratory animal research, the clinical entity is recognized and appropriately treated throughout the world.

As was often the custom with Dr. Peltier's residents, if you didn't already have a research study underway, you would probably be recruited to help on a new project. One research project that Dr. Peltier embarked upon during this time dealt with the safety of operating through a third-degree burn when internally fixing a fracture, usually of a long bone. The question arose, could this be done by covering the burned incision site at the time of wound closure with a skin graft, thus lessening the likelihood of a post-op wound infection? The protocol called for anesthetized rats to be the animal studied. The size and location of the burn site was controlled by use of a small template, and the third-degree burn was created by a small blowtorch. Well, this was not one of the more popular research projects among the residents, I can assure you! The aroma of burned flesh tends to be long-lasting, and on the days of his participation in the project, the involved resident was usually kept at arm's length when afternoon rounds were made. I regret to say, I am unable to accurately comment upon the outcome of this project today.

The academic instruction during these years included a Monday evening lecture by one of the three full-time staff members (Peltier, Litton, and Adler), although on rare occasions, an outside expert was enlisted. Additionally, each Saturday, promptly at 8 a.m., the week's X-ray conference took place. Frequently it was attended by several of the private town orthopedists. Here, in my judgment, Dr. Peltier's Socratic method of teaching medical students and house officers shone most brightly.

Upon completion of my training in June of 1964, I was offered a faculty position, along with Fred Reckling, who, under the Berry Plan, soon would enter the military service for two years. I chose to return to Denver, where my heart lay in the Rocky Mountain West. Fate then reappeared in the spring of 1972 in the form of a regional American Academy of Orthopaedic Surgeons' workshop on the use of a new cement, methylmethacrylate, that had been used for sometime in England to secure artificial hip implants. The FDA, in spite of the success in England, mandated that before any surgeon could use the cement, he or she needed to attend one of many regional laboratory workshops. I was involved as an instructor, having visited Mr. John Charnley in England in 1970 and having been granted one of the few FDA permits to use the cement clinically. Dr. Peltier attended the workshop, and the student now became the teacher. Dr. Peltier had moved to Tucson in 1971 where a new medical school and University Hospital had just been created. Shortly after our encounter at the workshop, I received a call asking if I might consider a move to Tucson to join the "Professor" in this new endeavor. After two visits to Tucson, and with the support of a caring and understanding wife, I accepted.

The Arizona Years

The decision to create a medical school in Arizona came about in the early 1960s with a small financial commitment by the State Legislature. An advisory committee of nationally respected physicians and academicians from other scientific disciplines was established to determine whether the school should be placed in the more centrally-located metropolitan area of Phoenix as a branch of Arizona State University (ASU) or further to the south in Tucson as a part of the University of Arizona (UA). Tucson was chosen as the medical school site, much to the anger of the Phoenix politicians and county medical association. The choice of Tucson was based upon the fact that UA possessed a more qualified science faculty that might serve as a valuable resource. The creation of the medical school in Tucson had been fought by many of the private community physicians who saw it as a threat to their practices. It was a tenuous "town-gown" relationship that would simmer below the surface for years to come. The 110-bed University Hospital opened on 1 September 1971.

At the time of Dr. Peltier's appearance on the scene, most of the department chairs had been recruited and filled by the newly appointed dean, Monty DuVal. Dr. DuVal had reached out across the country and had recruited some of the nation's leading academicians from schools such as Duke, Chapel Hill (University of North Carolina), Virginia, Case Western, and Stanford. Erle Peacock, chair of the UA Department of Surgery, had personally recruited Dr. Peltier to develop the Section of Orthopedic Surgery. Dr. Peltier reported directly to Dr. Peacock. In July of 1973, with my addition to the faculty, the number of full-time surgical faculty became twenty-six. Most of the faculty members recruited by Erle Peacock were personally known to him through academic circles. Most were young, quite scholarly, and unproven in building a busy clinical practice. Dr. Peltier, by contrast, was the oldest and the most proven faculty member in terms of developing a residency program, at the same time as maintaining a commitment to a busy clinical practice.

In the summer of 1973 I arrived to find a scarcity of patients, hospital beds under-utilized, and the operating room schedule usually completed by noon. A preoperative conference was held every day at 1 p.m., and Dr. Peacock believed that the faculty and resident staffs' presence should preempt most non-critical patient care. From my perspective, Erle Peacock chaired these conferences with an imperial, evangelistic and at times, manipulative manner. I was struck that, at times, the basic issues of a specific case were sidelined by impractical, esoteric diversions among his minions. The wise counsel of experienced clinicians often seemed to be lacking. The basic practicalities of treating ordinary fractures were usually the last of the concerns to be discussed.

It was also shortly after my arrival in Tucson that Erle Peacock was removed as the chair by Dean DuVal for reasons of a lack of collegiality with his fellow faculty heads, who nearly to a man encouraged and supported this decision. In taking this action, Peacock was not offered "due process" because Dean DuVal believed that department chairs served at his pleasure. A maelstrom was immediately set in process, as most of the surgical staff began to petition other faculty members to support their view that the dismissal was vindictive and uncalled for. The conflict grew and raged for nearly three years, at the expense of the school's image, both locally and nationally. There were frequent headlines in the Tucson papers about the internal strife at the medical school. Dr. John Schaefer, the university president, was publicly quoted as saying, "hell for a university president is having a medical school."

Dr. Peltier and I became the first to withdraw our support of Erle Peacock, a fight which was compromising the more important goals of resident recruitment and training, research and patient care. My response to Erle was that "I had not moved to Tucson to fight his political battles." Thus we stood two against twenty-four, with many unpleasant surgical colleague interchanges. A last ditch effort to bring the national office of the ACLU into the fray failed, and by 1976, Dr. Steve Wangensteen was made the new chair, with the subsequent departure of many of the malcontents. The "Peacock Affair," I believe, would not have happened in a more mature medical school with traditions and a higher commitment to the institution at large. I have no doubt that Dr. Peltier, in his quiet senior statesman's way, did much to swing the support from Erle's supporters to the school's best interest.

With the Peacock Affair behind us, the section began to grow, adding four new faculty members from Canada. The arrival of these new faculty members increased the section's expertise in orthopedic subspecialties. At the time of my arrival in Tucson, Dr. Peltier was not yet ready to accept the concept of specialization among the orthopedic staff. However, the most compelling reason for my decision to join the medical school was the perception that Arizona was not only in the "sun belt," but also in the arthritic belt. Convinced after a personal visit to Sir John Charnley in Wrightington, England, that total joints were on the threshold of further research and development, I pressed the "Professor" so that I could focus my efforts on the adult arthritic population. Thus began the creation of orthopedic specialization in the section. By 1977 the section offered specialty focuses of care in pediatrics, sports medicine, spine and hand care, in addition to general trauma.

At the same time as in- and out-patient populations grew rapidly, the residency program began to gain national attention. In 1974 I can recall eight applications for the one-per-year training position. By the late 1980s that number had grown to nearly 300 per year for two resident openings. No longer were the brightest medical school graduates applying to other specialties, such as internal medicine, for many had discovered the exciting breadth of dramatic care that orthopedic surgery offered.

The residency program continued to expand under the guidance of the "Professor," with the addition of several weekly conferences and a journal club. All residents were encouraged to carry out a meaningful research project, either of a clinical or a laboratory nature. A well-equipped biomechanics laboratory with an MTS (Materials Testing Systems) machine facilitated several studies that were reported in nationally recognized scientific journals. A full-time bioengineer had been hired, who also regularly offered bioengineering lectures to the resident staff. Yearly scholarly contributions were being made to the

Orthopaedic Research Society, and Donald Speer won the Hip Society's coveted John Charnley Award in 1982. The medical school was also garnering national recognition, and its hospital was consistently ranked among the nation's top teaching institutions. By 1985, Dr. Peltier decided to resign as section head but was soon called back into action as the Acting Head of the Department of Surgery following the departure of Dr. Wangensteen. Once again his leadership skills were called into action as the department searched for a new head and faculty stability. In 1990 Dr. Peltier retired from the university with several health problems and in 1997 moved to Albuquerque, New Mexico, to be near his son Stephen and family. With progressively failing eyesight, his ability to read and write gradually became compromised. Yet he continued to contribute historical articles to the journal of *Clinical Orthopaedics and Related Research*.

Ann and I would frequently visit Leonard and Marian as we passed through New Mexico. We always found the "Professor" with an uncomplaining optimistic outlook. The glass was always half-full for Leonard Peltier, no matter how steep the slope. Thus his favorite parting salutation, "onward and upward."

There are two men in my life that I owe much to: my father for his unending emotional and financial support during the long period of training as a surgeon, and Dr. Peltier who gave me the opportunity to become not only a surgeon, but to stand at his side for nineteen years while on staff at the University Hospital in Tucson. His gifts of knowledge, counsel and friendship shall remain cherished with me always.

— Robert G. Volz, M.D.
Professor Emeritus
Arizona Health Sciences Center

Preface

In 1996 while working at the University of Arizona, College of Medicine, I decided to write a book about Dr. Peltier. At that time very little had been done to record the biographies of the founding medical school faculty such as Dr. Peltier. From 1975-85, I worked in the orthopedic surgery section during the decade of its most rapid expansion. For six of those years, I was Dr. Peltier's administrative assistant and coordinated the orthopedic surgery residency program.

Dr. Peltier was a major influence in my life. I had many fond memories of those years as well as friendships with the former orthopedic residents. After I left the section, Dr. Peltier continued to be my friend. We exchanged Christmas cards, and he sent me flowers during a major health crisis. He frequently stopped by my office at the medical school to visit and also gave me autographed copies of his books.

In 1996 Dr. Peltier agreed to let me write his biography. Shortly before his move to Albuquerque, I interviewed him weekly for four months. Dr. Peltier provided me with access to the Peltier family newspaper and magazine clipping files, his curriculum vitae, and an unpublished memoir of his father which I had typed for Dr. Peltier many years previously.

I read many of his journal articles as well as historical files about the medical school and Dr. Erle Peacock at the medical school library and Arizona Historical Society. From 1997-99, I interviewed many former orthopedic residents, faculty, staff, and other colleagues who worked with Dr. Peltier in various roles.

As I began writing the manuscript, I called Dr. Peltier frequently to corroborate details. During one of these conversations, he expressed an interest in reading some letters I received from the former orthopedic residents. I decided to solicit as many letters as I could get and attach

Readers will note that initials are used throughout the text to denote a few of the individuals who are mentioned most frequently, particularly LFP. This was a convention that he frequently employed, following the example of his mentor Owen H. Wangensteen (OHW). You will see Janolyn G. Lo Vecchio (JGL), Frederick W. Reckling (FWR) and JoAnn B. Reckling (JBR) referred to in a similar fashion.

It will also be noticed that two differing spellings: "orthopedics" and "orthopaedics" are used. "Proper" or "preferred" spelling of the word has been a long-time topic of discussion,* and in most cases, LFP opted for the simpler spelling (notice the title of one of his books: *Orthopedics: A History and Iconography*). The origin of the *ae* combination, a dipthong (two letters attached together), is derived from the Greek spelling of "*pai*dion" (child), which was paired with "orthos," (straight and free from deformity). Nicolas Andry used the French *ae* instead of *ai* when he coined the word ortho*pae*dic, and many of the professional organizations and journals retain that language. However, in most situations, modern usage has discarded the dipthong in preference to the individual letter: for example pediatrics instead of p*ae*diatrics. Following the lead of LFP, the authors elected to use the "*e*," rather than the "*ae*" spelling whenever they were not directly quoting an individual, journal, or organization that used, or uses, the *ae* option.

Given that orthopedics literally means "straight child," it is easy to recall that the original focus of orthopedists was the treatment of a variety of deformities. LFP wrote extensively about the development of the specialty, and the small figures of "cripples" that are placed throughout this book are used with the permission of Norman Publishing, from the frontispiece of LFP's *Orthopedics: A History and Iconography*. The frontispiece of this biography of LFP includes his explanation of the derivation and evolution of the term "cripple" from accepted to pejorative language.

*Howorth, Beckett, M.D., "Orthopaedics [vs. Orthopedics]," letter, *Clinical Orthopaedics and Related Research*, 118 (July-August 1976): 270-1.

The publication lists at the end of chapters were derived from LFP's curriculum vitae. It will be noted that he did not include many of his nearly 200 "introductions" to Classics Articles in *Clinical Orthopaedics and Related Research*.

The cost of this publication was privately funded by the authors. Should any proceeds be derived from book distribution, they will be applied to the Leonard F. Peltier Lectureship or the Peltier/Reckling Alumni Professor and Chair of Orthopedic Surgery at the University of Kansas School of Medicine.

We are not professional biographers, and if errors, understatements, or oversights have occurred, despite our best efforts, we accept responsibility for them. Most importantly, our goal for this biography has been to document the life and career of an extraordinary man in an accurate, readable, and interesting way.

— FREDERICK W. RECKLING
JOANN B. RECKLING

Acknowledgments

ॐ

We wish to acknowledge the many individuals, teaching institutions, and professional societies that have contributed verbal, written and visual information incorporated in *Onward and Upward: the Career Trajectory and Memories of Leonard F. Peltier, M.D, Ph.D.* We especially want to thank the Peltier family for their enthusiastic support for the project. Their authentication of facts and dates, provision of information in the form of Dr. Peltier's pertinent personal papers, allowing us to reproduce priceless family photographs, and answers to a myriad of questions greatly facilitated and enhanced our efforts to include a family perspective in this biography.

Phone conversations, audiotapes and written communications from many residents trained by LFP at the University of Kansas, including Federico Adler, Howard Ellfeldt, James Glenn, Wallace Holderman, Samuel Kaplan, James Laidlaw, W. Robert Orr, John Pazell, Melvin Roberts, Robert Volz and John Wertzberger, provided insight into LFP's early years as a program chief. Similarly, former LFP residents at the University of Arizona, including James Benjamin, Keith Braun, James Bried, John Brugman, Dwite Dahms, Ernest Gradillas, Ralph Heap, Robert Karpman, John Kloss, Richard Laubengayer, Joseph Nichols, Thomas Peters, Donald Speer, and Francisco Valencia, offered information about the Arizona years. Laurel Speer touchingly recalled LFP's care and concern for the families of his residents and associates.

Former administrators and faculty associates at the University of Kansas Medical Center (KUMC), including Federico Adler, James Basham, W. David Francisco, Stanley Friesen, and Frank Masters, commented upon LFP's early academic career at KU from a faculty perspective, while James Benjamin, Milos Chvapil, James Dalen, George Drach, Robert Dzioba, Warren Eddy, Gordon Ewy, Frederick

Greenwood, Philip Krutzsch, E. C. Percy, Michael Pitt, Donald Speer and Robert Volz provided information and vignettes from a faculty viewpoint about LFP's tenure at the University of Arizona Health Sciences Center (AHSC). Colleagues from across the nation, J. Bradley Aust, Carl Brighton, C. Rollins Hanlon, George Sheldon and Marshall Urist, shared their insight into LFP's national impact on medical education.

Administrative and secretarial staff members at AHSC and the Tucson Veterans Administration (VA) Hospital, including Susie Brandes, Carolyn Kelsey, Esther Ochoa and Cheryl Zimmer supplied testimony regarding the effectiveness of LFP's administrative style. Deborah Dodge shared memories of working with Dr. Peltier as his orthopedic clinic nurse and commented on his respect for and appreciation of nurses, while Anna Sherlock wrote about LFP's acknowledgement of the importance of hospital support staff.

W. Brandon Wright, M.D., scientific investigator at the University of Pennsylvania, expressed appreciation for his training in LFP's orthopedic lab at KUMC. Marian Kuenzig, LFP's laboratory technician at KUMC, contributed insightful information regarding his approach into scientific laboratory investigations.

One time KU graphic artist, Beverly Brewster Sherrell, related how she worked with LFP in creating the "crooked sunflower" and "crooked cactus" logos and explained their subtle representations. She further shared poignant information about his broad life interests.

Personnel in the library information services at AHSC provided details regarding LFP's knowledge and proficiency in the use of the medical literature, written in many different languages. Hannah Fisher, Fred Heidenreich, Mary Riordan and especially Nga Nguyen, had worked closely with LFP as he gathered data for his many scientific and literary contributions.

As development of the manuscript progressed, people from a number of organizations assisted us with finding images and granting us permission to use them. We thank Amy Bordiuk, Managing Editor, and Mady Tissenbaum, General Manager, of the *Journal of Bone and Joint Surgery*; Elaine Challacombe, Curator of the Wangensteen

Historical Library, University of Minnesota, and Karen Klinkenberg, of the University of Minnesota Archives; Linn Meyer, Director of Communications at the American College of Surgeons; Jeremy Norman and Martha Steele of the Norman Publishing Company; David O'Brien, Copyright & Communications Coordinator of Lippincott, Williams & Wilkins *(Annals of Surgery, Clinical Orthopaedics and Related Research, Journal of Trauma* and *Little, Brown and Company)*; the University of Arizona Foundation; Jan Davis of the University of Arizona Library and Archives; Carolyn Robinson of Manley-Prim Photography, Inc. in Tucson; The University of Arizona Biomedical Communications Department of the Arizona College of Medicine; the University of Arizona Department of Surgery; and Felipe Jacome, Director of the Gallery in the Sun, Tucson, Arizona, who granted us permission to reproduce a copy of De Grazia's Cabeza de Vaca painting entitled "Operation Arrowhead." Additionally, Fred Adler, Brad Aust, Jim Benjamin, and Milos Chvapil provided photographs from their personal collections for use in the biography. Fred Adler, Brad Aust, Jim Benjamin, Carl Brighton, Milos Chvapil, Carolyn Kelsey, Nga Nguyen, Bob Volz and several members of the Peltier family shared information about LFP's later years.

Throughout the process of gathering supplemental material and editing the manuscript, a number of individuals have provided invaluable assistance, often on a somewhat urgent time line. Susie Brandes, Nga Nguyen, and Cheryl Zimmer at the AHSC were particularly helpful to the authors in securing information and clarifying details. There were occasions when we needed aid in identifying individuals in photographs, as well as securing information about them. Jean and Dave Francisco, along with Marian Peltier, assisted us in identifying Mrs. James Weaver. Bob Hudson, with his exhaustive knowledge of medical and KU history, answered our questions with substantive data and good humor! Fred Adler was always willing to respond to a request, read a chapter, offer a photo, a book, an audiotape, and simply be available when we needed a sounding board for a particular facet of the biography. He knew LFP so well!

Benita Bobbitt and Jane Tugurian of Vanderbilt University supplied us with information about Vernon Wilson, after Fred Adler and Bob Hudson had probed their memories of times long-past and verified his identity. Bernie Albina and Arlo Hermreck joined us in our unsuccessful quest to identify a surgery resident in a photo in the Kansas chapter. Vertis Walker supplied us with demographic information about the American Association for the Surgery of Trauma. And Cary Hagan of Wright Medical Technology, Inc., verified scientific information about the current status of antibiotic-impregnated plaster of Paris.

Fred Adler, Chuck and Nancy Bell, Jim Benjamin, Milos Chvapil, Bob Hudson, Nga Nguyen, and Bob Volz, as well as Marian Peltier, and George and Steve Peltier and their families, took the time and energy to review early drafts of the entire manuscript and make valuable suggestions and corrections.

The University of Kansas Clendening History of Medicine Library and Museum is sponsoring publication of the book. We want to thank the library staff, including Chris Crenner, Nancy Hulston, Dawn McInnis and others, who graciously and generously supplied vital information, photos and digital reproduction expertise. Mary Ann Booth, Coordinator of KUMC Alumni and Community Relations, was helpful in looking for information in the KUMC *Jayhawker* yearbooks. Chuck Cordt of the KU Endowment Association assisted us with financial arrangements.

We also extend a special thanks to Marc Asher and Bruce Toby, who not only gave us their heartfelt encouragement throughout the writing and publishing process, but were indispensable in coordinating our efforts with the Department of Orthopedic Surgery at KU, Clendening History of Medicine Library, and Payson Lowell of Greystone Graphics where the book was printed. In addition to helpful advice about the intricacies of preparing a book for printing, selecting paper and cover materials, and facilitating plans for book distribution, Payson has worked closely with Dawn McInnis of the Clendening Library assisting her in securing ISBN and Library of Congress numbers.

Carol Stevens of Lynx Design, Laramie, WY, has been indispensable with her creative suggestions and many hours dedicated to designing and illustrating the book. We are deeply indebted to Carol and Payson Lowell for their advice and "know-how" regarding the transformation of a manuscript into a finished product!

And last, but certainly not least, we extend a special thanks to Bob Volz, who has been helpful throughout the process, encouraging the authors at the outset, providing further insight into LFP's years at the University of Arizona, supplying information as the manuscript was in process, reviewing it, and graciously adding an additional dimension with his insightful Foreword.

—Janolyn G. Lo Vecchio
Frederick W. Reckling
JoAnn B. Reckling

Leonard F. Peltier, M.D., Ph.D.
1920-2003

∾

Professional Organizations and Societies

Alpha Omega Alpha (Kansas), American Academy of Orthopaedic Surgeons, American Association for the History of Medicine, American Association for the Surgery of Trauma, American College of Surgeons, American Surgical Association, Arizona Medical Association, Association of Bone and Joint Surgeons (honorary member), Association of Orthopaedic Chairmen, Institute of Accident Surgery (Birmingham, England), International Society of Orthopaedic Surgery and Traumatology (S.I.C.O.T.), Orthopaedic Research Society, Pima County Medical Society, Sigma Xi, Society for Experimental Biology and Medicine, Society of University Surgeons, The Halsted Society, The Hunterian Society (London, England), Western Orthopaedic Association.

Leonard F. Peltier Career Chronology

ॐ

Nebraska

1920 — **Born in Wisconsin Rapids, Wisconsin (January 1920)**
Capitol Elementary School, Lincoln, Nebraska

1930 —
Irving Junior High School, Lincoln, Nebraska
Lincoln High School, Lincoln, Nebraska (graduated 1937)
National Honor Society
Regents Scholarship Contest (honorable mention)

1940 —
A.B., University of Nebraska (June 1941)

Minnesota

Married Marian K. (November 1943)
M.D., University of Minnesota (1944)*
Straight surgical internship, University of Minnesota (1944-5)
General surgery residency, University of Minnesota (July 1945-March 1946)
    until interrupted by military service
U.S. Army (March 1946-August 1948)
General surgery residency, University of Minnesota (July 1948-September
    1950)

1950 —
Research Fellow, Department of Physiology, University of Minnesota
    (October 1950-June 1951)
National Foundation for Infantile Paralysis Fellowship (1950-1)
Ph.D. (Major in Surgery, Minor in Physiology), University of Minnesota
    (1951)
John and Mary R. Markle Scholar in Medical Science (1952-6)
Clinical Instructor, Department of Surgery, University of Minnesota (1951-3)
Orthopedic surgery residency, University of Minnesota (July 1951-June
    1952) and Gillette State Hospital for Crippled Children (July 1952-
    June 1953)
    Diplomate, American Board of Surgery (1954)
    Diplomate, American Board of Orthopaedic Surgery (1956)
Clinical Assistant Professor, Department of Surgery, Division of Orthopedic
    Surgery, University of Minnesota (1953-6)
Associate Professor and Acting Head, Division of Orthopedic Surgery,
    University of Minnesota (July-December 1956)

---

* The actual degree awarded in 1944 was that of Bachelor of Medicine. At that time in the State of Minnesota it was possible to go into practice immediately following graduation without serving an internship. In order to insure that all of its graduates completed an internship, the University of Minnesota did not grant the M.D. until the following year. This was done automatically. This system was abandoned soon after his class graduated. As a result, LFP always listed his M.D. as being awarded in 1944.

Kansas

Professor of Surgery and Chairman, Section of Orthopedic Surgery, University of Kansas College of Medicine (January 1957-June 1971)

Kappa Delta Award, American Academy of Orthopaedic Surgeons (January 1957)

1960 — Editorial board member and Consultant, *Surgery* (1960-70)

Nicolas Andry Award, Association of Bone and Joint Surgery (1961)

Consulting editor, *Journal of Surgical Oncology* (1969-90)

1970 —

Arizona

Professor of Surgery and Section Chief, Orthopedic Surgery, University of Arizona College of Medicine (July 1971-June 1985)

Chief of Orthopedic Surgery, Veterans Administration Medical Center, Tucson, Arizona (July 1971-June 1983)

American College of Surgeons Committees:

Committee on trauma (1972-81)

Committee on post-graduate education (1972-82)

Consultant, *Journal of Trauma* (1972-2003)

Consultant, *Journal of Bone and Joint Surgery*

American Association for the Surgery of Trauma, Board of Managers (1975-83)

Acting Chief of Surgery, Veterans Administration Medical Center, Tucson, Arizona (1975-7)

Acting Head, Department of Surgery, University of Arizona College of Medicine (1 July 1976 – 30 September 1976)

Clinical Orthopaedics and Related Research Board of Advisory Editors (1978-2003), Deputy Editor (Classics) (1979-2003)

1980 — American Association for the Surgery of Trauma, President (1980-1)

American College of Surgeons, Board of Governors (1980-6); Vice-Chairman of that board (1984-6)

Acting Head, Department of Surgery, University of Arizona College of Medicine (1986-90)

American Academy of Orthopaedic Surgeons, Committee on the History of Orthopaedics (1989-93), Chairman (1992)

1990 — Professor Emeritus of Orthopedic Surgery, University of Arizona College of Medicine (July 1990)

Peltier Lectureship, University of Kansas School of Medicine (1994)

New Mexico

2000 — **Died in Rochester, Minnesota (4 May 2003)**

Peltier/Reckling Alumni Professor and Chair of Orthopedic Surgery, University of Kansas School of Medicine (2004)

CHAPTER ONE

Heritage, Youth and Early Education

"If I were writing my autobiography, I would say that I have been a very fortunate person who had disappointments and successes, and an interesting career."

— LEONARD F. PELTIER (LFP)[1]

∾*T*he name Peltier, translated into English, means furrier. This might create a mental image of the *coureur du bois* (woodsman) trekking through the Canadian wilderness in pursuit of fur-bearing animals. However, the name does not accurately characterize the Peltier family. Actually, LFP's ancestors were small farmers near Quebec City, Canada. Some of the sons emigrated to the United States, including LFP's paternal grandfather (Emile A. Peltier), who settled in Wisconsin.

LFP elaborated: "My grandfather [Emile] was a millwright who played the organ in the local Catholic Church. Two of my uncles were gassed in World War I and later died from pulmonary diseases related to the gassing. All of my remaining uncles were successful small businessmen. My father, George L. Peltier, grew up in a French-Canadian ghetto in a sawmill town in Wisconsin."[2]

Although LFP's father, George, grew up the son of a logger in Wisconsin, he became an academician. George described his upbringing in his unpublished memoir, *This I Remember*.[3] "My father [LFP's paternal grandfather, Emile], who lived in Merrill, Wisconsin, worked in logging camps in the north woods as a timber scaler. He also was very proficient with figures, although he had no formal schooling. He could add up a long column of figures faster than a machine and likewise could estimate the total number of board feet in a towering lumber pile simply by looking at it. My mother [LFP's paternal grandmother, Georgiana L. Peltier] received the equivalent of a third grade education, but can be characterized as the best manager in existence. It is quite remarkable how she, with very modest means, brought up a family of ten independent children. She was not only a resourceful, but an independent and prideful person."

French was George's first language, and he did not speak English until he went to school, but he became a voracious reader, even as a young boy. "I was the oldest of the ten children and did have chores to do. Filling the wood box each evening was a sort of ritual. Above the wood box was a bracket kerosene lamp with a large reflector that served to illuminate the stove area and provided enough light for me to read. After supper my perch atop the wood box was my evening retreat. Here, out of the way of my busy mother and my younger bothersome brothers, with book in hand, I lived and dreamed of heroes and explored the vast unknown. Never will I forget those golden moments back of the stove. Those were the happiest moments of my life, perched on the wood box.

"The local library was also one of my cherished resorts from the age of six upward. At one time I managed to read at least six books a week. For some unknown reason I always enjoyed school. The one and only text that I still cherish and enjoy from my grade school years is entitled *Word Building*, by Kellog and Reed, 1899. This text, which I still refer to, has probably made a more profound impression on me than any other text I ever studied.

"In 1901, the year I started high school, our family moved to Centralia, Wisconsin, now Wisconsin Rapids. The town was a wood-working center with a sawmill, a sash and door factory, a box factory, a hub and spoke mill, two furniture factories, a small pulp mill, a small foundry and a flour and feed mill. The population of 4,500 was made up of lumber barons, French-Canadians, first-generation Germans,

Swedes and Poles. The two dominant [religious] denominations were Catholics and Lutherans."

George was the first person in his French-Canadian community to attend college and obtain advanced degrees. During his high school years, teachers influenced him to consider attending the university, something to which he had given little thought. "The only opposition I ever had from Dad was when I determined to go to the university. In going through his belongings after his death, I did find a worn-out clipping regarding my appointment to my first job [Auburn University], so that I learned for the first time that perhaps deep down in his heart he felt that I had done the right thing in seeking an education."

Having grown up with the smell of the forests, George decided that forestry would be a fine profession. He entered the University of Wisconsin in 1905. His tuition for the first year was only $17.50, and his expenses for the first year totaled $210. He waited tables and worked in labs during the school year and worked other jobs during the summers to earn money for his education, but money was always scarce. The local bank president loaned him $300 for each of his last three years. He had the opportunity to work during his college years in botany research projects, including a study of cranberry diseases. After graduating from the university in 1909 with a B. A. degree in botany, he taught in the high school in Wauwatosa, Wisconsin, a suburb of Milwaukee, for two years before continuing his postgraduate education at the Botanical Gardens in St. Louis, Missouri. LFP recalled the family story: "During the long period of schooling necessary for my dad to obtain his B.A. and Ph.D. degrees, a neighbor leaning across the fence to talk with his mother [LFP's grandmother] said: 'George will go to school so long he'll be a fool.'"

In September 1913, during his graduate study years, George married Florence "Floy" L. Quinn, a librarian whom he had met in Wisconsin Rapids. In 1915 he received his Ph.D. in Plant Pathology from the University of Illinois, Urbana, and he and Floy then moved to Auburn, Alabama, where he founded a new Department of Plant Pathology at Auburn University. Their first child, Marjorie I. (Sally) Peltier was born in 1915.

In 1920 the Peltiers moved to Lincoln, Nebraska, where Dr. George Peltier became the head of the Department of Plant Pathology at the University of Nebraska. During the move, Floy returned to her mother's home in Wisconsin Rapids, Wisconsin, where LFP was born

George L. Peltier, Ph.D.
1888-1975
∽
Professor Peltier evaluating laboratory specimen, circa 1942.

Photo courtesy of the Peltier family

in January 1920. According to George, "Floy's mother [Helen "Nellie" B. Quinn, LFP's maternal grandmother] had completed a high-school education, was well-read, could recite quotes from Shakespeare, and...could do many things very well."

Thus, LFP grew up in an academic setting, with a variety of scholarly influences, among people who loved books. LFP remembered: "My father was a hard working man who was interested in gardening, flowers, and plants. Although he had a sense of humor, he lived within himself and was not an extrovert. He was a bacteriologist as well as a plant pathologist. He worked thirty-three years for the University of Nebraska. He had the first climate-controlled greenhouses in the United States. They were built in 1927 when there was an outbreak of alfalfa wilt in the Platte River valley. He received a special appropriation from the state legislature to build the greenhouses to do research on [this agriculture-threatening disease]. The greenhouses were equipped with a freezing chamber and central temperature controls. He developed strains of wilt-resistant alfalfa as well as strains with enhanced winter hardiness." His father published more than 120 articles and wrote two books during his career.

"My mother had a good sense of humor. My mother and father were an average young couple in the 1920s who enjoyed playing cards and attending dances promoted by the faculty. Lincoln, Nebraska, at that time was a town of 40,000, with little or no industry. Instead it had the state capitol, the university, the state penitentiary, and the state insane asylum. Crime was essentially non-existent, and it was safe for children to ride their bicycles all over town."

As a child, LFP had opportunities to stay in touch with his Wisconsin relatives, although travel could be an adventure. In 1926, when LFP was six years old, his parents bought a used Studebaker touring car and traveled to Wisconsin to visit relatives, a three-day drive over unpaved roads. "There was no air-conditioning, and it was quite breezy. There were side curtains that were very difficult to use, and a luggage rack attached to the running board. My mother carried a yardstick that could reach into all corners of the back seat. She used it to maintain discipline between brother and sister. We traveled with our big dog, Lucky. Gas stations still pumped gas by hand at five gallons for a dollar. We had frequent punctures and blowouts. To fix a tire you had to take the inner tube out, find the hole in it and vulcanize a patch on it, and then pump the tire up again. There were few paved roads and no motels. We packed our own food and stayed at 'homes for tourists' or 'cabin camps.'"

At the age of ten, LFP contracted rheumatic fever, an event that radically changed his active childhood, due to the hours of rest required for convalescence. "It made me into a couch potato because athletics were out." He developed a love of reading and collected fossils, arrowheads and all sorts of odds and ends.

The Great Depression hit hard, but although the state cut all of the university salaries by twenty-five percent, the Peltiers considered themselves lucky. Many of the fathers in the neighborhood had lost their jobs. The Peltiers did not live in University Place where most of the academic faculty lived, but instead, lived in the central city. LFP's sister played the violin, and he played the trumpet and bass horn and also sang in the choir. In his senior year in high school, LFP became a member of the National Honor Society and received honorable mention in the Regent's Scholarship Contest. He graduated from Lincoln High School in a class of 700 students on 9 June 1937. That fall, he enrolled as a freshman at the University of Nebraska.

"I was able to obtain one of the unclaimed Regent's Scholarships. As a result I paid no tuition during my freshman year. This was particularly important because 1937 was the very bottom of the Depression. I attended college where my father was a professor. On the first day of classes when the roll was called, teachers would pause and look around to see who I was [obviously wishing to identify the son of one of their colleagues]. I took a psychology class that I did not attend after the first day because it was a 'snap' course. At a faculty meeting the professor asked my father if I had dropped his course. After that, my father told me to go to class and I did."

LFP joined three college fraternities: Sigma Chi (social), Sinfonia (musical), and Theta Nu (pre-med). "I was initiated into Sigma Chi after 'hell week,' which consisted primarily of sleep deprivation. I was kept awake for three days waxing floors and washing windows. I did not fall asleep because I was kept too busy. The fraternity was a valuable experience for me because it taught me how to work with people, developed my personal relationship skills, and 'smoothed' me up in manners and dress. Although I was a town boy who lived at home, I frequently visited the fraternity house for meals, card games, etc. The house mother did not tolerate misbehavior or slovenly dress."

Because the University of Nebraska was a land grant college, LFP was required to "take ROTC" (be a member of the Reserve Officer's Training Corp) for two years, an experience that he loathed. "You had to wear a uniform to school one day a week and march around the campus carrying a rifle. It was 1938 and money was scarce. Advanced ROTC paid a small stipend, which was a good deal of money in those days. I took advanced ROTC and went to summer camp at old Fort Crook south of Omaha. This later became Offutt Air Force Base, the home of the Strategic Air Command. The ROTC unit consisted of an infantry regiment and an artillery regiment. The military ceremonies on the campus involved a substantial number of students. I was assigned the job of being the aide to the chancellor of the university. When the chancellor participated in the military ceremonies, I was at his side, explaining events. It gave me the opportunity to develop self-confidence. The fraternity and the ROTC provided me with very important college experiences. When I graduated from the university, I received a Bachelor of Arts degree as well as a commission as a Second Lieutenant in the U.S. Army infantry reserves."

When LFP was a freshman in college he was interested in basic sciences, but a career in that area soon lost its luster, causing him to consider another profession. "After studying chemistry and other [laboratory] sciences, I became aware of, and despised, the plight of the postgraduate students in the basic sciences. I became determined never to become a [laboratory science] graduate student. The only other option was medicine."

In 1940 LFP met his wife-to-be, Marian, another student at the University of Nebraska. "I had been dating a girl who became president of Mortar Board, and when we broke up I needed a date, as all of my friends had steady girlfriends. Two of my fraternity brothers sat down with me with the college yearbook to see if there was an Alpha Phi who I might take out. Marian, a sophomore, was one of the few who were not going steady. She was the daughter of an Omaha surgeon and was studying to become a hospital dietitian. It took quite a while to get a date with her, because she had other boyfriends and refused to go out with me until we had met. Our first date was an afternoon meeting over Cokes. In the spring of 1941 things got pretty serious, and we had a pinning ceremony, followed by a serenade. A few months later we became officially engaged.

Although LFP's parents did not react strongly to the news that he planned to become a doctor, he knew that his maternal grandmother, Helen, would have been very pleased. She had always hoped he would become one, like her favorite brother, who was an eye doctor. LFP did not want to attend medical school at the University of Nebraska because he did not want to be pointed out as a professor's son for another four years. Fortunately, another alternative was the University of Minnesota Medical School. It was there that he would encounter Owen H. Wangensteen, M.D., Ph.D.,[4] Chairman of the Department of Surgery, who would become his lifelong professional role model.

Notes and Sources

1. Leonard F. Peltier often referred to himself as LFP in written communications. The authors will use these initials frequently throughout the text.

2. The personal statements by LFP throughout this book were made during interviews with Janolyn G. Lo Vecchio, Arizona Health Sciences Center, Tucson, AZ, as well as when he edited and added to JGL's original manuscript.

3. George L. Peltier, *This I Remember*, unpublished autobiography.

4. Owen Harding Wangensteen, M.D., Ph.D., renowned long-time Chairman of the Department of Surgery at the University of Minnesota, is a legend in himself. According to LFP and J. Bradley Aust, co-authors of *L'Étoile du Nord: An Account of Owen Harding Wangensteen (1898-1981)* (Chicago: American College of Surgeons, 1994), p. ix, Dr. Wangensteen was a man of many facets: "surgeon, scientist, educator, administrator, historian, and humanist."

CHAPTER TWO

The University of Minnesota

"Anyone in Owen H. Wangensteen's surgical residency program had knowingly chosen to be trained by him, not only because of his reputation, but also because of his emphasis on research in investigative surgery. He trained and created more professors of surgery than any other man or program in the United States."

— STANLEY R. FRIESEN, M.D., PH.D. [1]
PROFESSOR EMERITUS OF SURGERY AND
THE HISTORY AND PHILOSOPHY OF MEDICINE
UNIVERSITY OF KANSAS SCHOOL OF MEDICINE

"Owen's operation [the surgical residency at Minnesota] is reminiscent of a tunnel: trainees pour in one end; what they do in the tunnel we do not know, but we do see them emerge at the other end well-qualified and talented surgeons."

— OSCAR CREECH, JR., M.D. [2]
PROFESSOR AND CHAIRMAN
DEPARTMENT OF SURGERY
TULANE UNIVERSITY

*⬿L*FP entered the University of Minnesota (UM) Medical School in the fall of 1941 after an admission process that varied somewhat from the norm. "My parents had been good friends with the president of the University of Minnesota. I traveled to Minneapolis for a meeting with him. After a short interview, he picked up the phone and called the dean of the medical school, saying there was a young man in his office

that he should meet. I interviewed with the dean, took the MCAT [Medical College Admission Test] examination, and was admitted to the medical school at the University of Minnesota."

The UM Medical School was among the best in the country. The Elliott Memorial Hospital, dedicated in Minneapolis in September, 1911, was the first major teaching hospital unit of what eventually became the UM Medical Center.[3] It had 120 beds, forty of which were for surgical patients. The concept and character of this hospital were influenced by Abraham Flexner's 1909 review of the UM Medical School.[4] The Carnegie Foundation had commissioned Flexner, an educator, to evaluate the American system of producing physicians, and the resultant Flexner Report, published in 1910, was one of the most important documents in the history of American and Canadian medical

Elliott Memorial Hospital, University of Minnesota, 1950

∾

The white square building on the left was a temporary building nicknamed "the pillbox." Note the 1940s-vintage cars!

Photo courtesy of the University of Minnesota Archives

education. It focused on, and criticized, facilities and curricula of medical schools, and made recommendations for change. The Flexner Report triggered much-needed reforms in the standards, organization, and curricula of North American medical schools.[5]

Also in response to the Flexner Report, George Edgar Vincent, the president of UM from 1911-7, strengthened the medical faculty in 1914 by appointing Elias Potter Lyon, Ph.D., as dean of UM Medical School.[6] This appointment was controversial, as Dean Lyon's doctorate and professional expertise were in biology and physiology. His lack of a medical degree was a matter of consternation for some of the medical faculty. However, when he retired in 1936, he was lauded because the quality of the faculty members he had recruited had transformed the UM Medical School from a clinical program with only "moderate" scientific background to one of the top ten medical schools in the United States, both clinically and scientifically.[7]

One of Dean Lyon's first accomplishments, with the support of President Vincent, was formalizing a relationship between the UM Medical School in Minneapolis and the Mayo Clinic in Rochester, Minnesota, for the purpose of granting postgraduate academic degrees in medical disciplines. At that time standardized graduate education in clinical medicine (e.g., a residency program) was nonexistent. While some institutions, such as the Mayo Clinic, provided a number of years of well-rounded training to their Fellows, others provided a certificate after a few months' apprenticeship. "Specialists" could simply proclaim their expertise and begin practicing with little or no training beyond medical school. The University of Minnesota was initiating a formal three-year postgraduate training course for physicians to study with selected members of the medical faculty, under the supervision of the UM Graduate School. Those who completed the program would emerge with degrees such as a Ph.D. in Surgery, or an M.S. in Pediatrics.[8]

The Mayo Clinic organization favored the formation of an affiliation, as it would allow their Fellows an opportunity for additional scientific education. The Mayo Foundation for Medical Education and Research was formed especially for the purpose of making this affiliation possible. The Mayo brothers, William J. Mayo, M.D., and Charles H.

Mayo, M.D., endowed the fund, transferring personal securities worth one and one-half million dollars to provide money for the research and educational phases of the work.

The negotiation process to develop the partnership between the Mayo Clinic and UM was delicate. During the negotiations, William J. Mayo, M.D., was a member of the Board of Governors of the Mayo Clinic Foundation, as well as a member of the Board of Regents of UM. The state's medical community opposed a direct affiliation between the two institutions, fearing that the university might succumb to influences of privatization. Many were wary of the impact of potential competition from such a large organization upon their private practices. Some members of the UM Medical School faculty feared that the graduate school might overshadow the medical school in its influence on the education of young physicians. Furthermore, they were concerned about spreading their students geographically into two locations, possibly diminishing the quality of their education.[9]

In 1915 agreement was finally reached between the Board of Regents of UM and the Mayo Foundation, permitting Fellows of the Foundation with proper qualifications to obtain postgraduate degrees from the university. The agreement stipulated that students earning postgraduate degrees in medicine and surgery from the university and from the Mayo Clinic were matriculated through the UM Graduate School instead of the UM Medical School. Candidates for postgraduate study had to have completed their medical degrees and a year of internship. Three years of further study qualified them for a Doctor of Philosophy degree in their selected clinical subject. The outcome of this arrangement benefited departments and students in both institutions. Maintaining separation between the medical departments of the university and those of the Mayo Clinic allowed the Department of Surgery at UM to grow without interference from, or domination by, the Mayo Clinic. Additionally, the research undertaken by the residents was of a quality that would meet the requirements of the medical and the non-medical academic faculty of the university.[10] The requirements for the Ph.D. degree in a medical discipline were the same as for any other Ph.D. degree: proficiency in two foreign languages, a preliminary and a final oral examination, and a thesis. Examination committee members were chosen equally from the faculties of the university and the Mayo Clinic.[11]

During the decade following World War I, in response to the Flexner Report and as a result of Dean Lyons' recruiting, the faculty of the medical school gradually changed from part-time teachers to full-time professors. Owen H. Wangensteen (OHW), M.D., Ph.D., was one of these new faculty members. He earned his M.D. in 1921 and his Ph.D. in Surgery in 1925, both from UM. His training included rotations at the Mayo Clinic and Hennepin County Medical Center as well as the university hospital. He joined the faculty at UM immediately after his postgraduate training. He became Chairman of the Department of Surgery at UM in 1930, and a full professor in 1931.

LFP's first encounter with OHW "occurred when Dr. Wangensteen, a bright young man, about 45 years old, with an impressive manner, presented a case in the correlation clinic for the freshmen students. These clinics were designed to remind freshmen medical students that they would become doctors someday, and physicians from the different medical disciplines presented cases [to us] on a rotating basis."

Owen H. Wangensteen, M.D., Ph.D.
1898-1981

∾

Photo courtesy of the American College of Surgeons

During that same year, the United States entered World War II. The war created huge changes for the medical school. "In 1941, the dean of UM Medical School was called to Washington and put on a health committee. For the next three years the medical school was run by his secretary, who fulfilled the dean's job. She was even given the title 'Dean Smith' and was called Dean Smith by the faculty. Junior faculty and senior residents were also heavily recruited into the armed forces. As a result, the medical school and university hospital were manned by junior residents and local retired physicians."

LFP had been commissioned as a Second Lieutenant in the United States Army infantry reserves when he graduated from the University of Nebraska in 1941. In the fall of 1942, as more men were needed by the military, the United States War Department lowered the draft age from twenty-one to eighteen, although they recognized that this action would cut off the supply of college-trained men. They could neither afford the luxury of allowing a large proportion of the nation's military manpower to spend four years engaged in studies not vital to the war effort, nor could they afford to destroy their source of college-educated specialists for particular military positions.[12] They therefore undertook an ambitious military college training program that included undergraduate and professional graduate education. As part of this program, LFP was transferred into the Medical Administrative Corps (MAC) in 1942 and became a part of the Army Specialized Training Program (ASTP). Special provisions were made for medical, dental, and veterinary students who held commissions in the MAC to ensure that they could continue their training without being called to active duty, and that there would be no financial discrimination against them. The government was funding the education of premedical and predental students who were in the Enlisted (non-officer) Reserve Corps. In order to provide a similar arrangement at a similar pay grade, Reserve Officers such as LFP who were already enrolled in professional schools, were offered the opportunity to resign their commissions and enlist as privates to continue their studies at government expense. LFP took advantage of this opportunity, resigned his commission as a Second Lieutenant in the Reserves, and became a Private First Class in the ASTP. When he graduated from medical school, he was commissioned as a First Lieutenant in the Medical Corps.

When LFP began his medical education in 1941, sulfonamides had just been introduced, ending the pre-antibiotic era, and penicillin became available in 1944-45. Poliomyelitis was still a major problem. One memorable lecture at the medical school was given by the redoubtable Sister Kenny, the Australian nurse who revolutionized the treatment of acute polio cases. LFP recalled: "Dr. Wallace H. Cole, the chief of orthopedics at the university, had given Sister Kenny the opportunity to introduce her methods in Minneapolis. She was a very keen observer of her patients, but because she had little formal medical training, doctors had a hard time understanding the terminology that she used to describe them. Sister Kenny was a formidable presence and always was accompanied by a large entourage of her therapists. One day Sister Kenny was scheduled to lecture to our class of sophomore medical students. On the day of her lecture, Sister Kenny's technicians came into the amphitheater and occupied the front rows. When Sister Kenny arrived, all of her technicians stood up respectfully. The medical students continued to lounge in their chairs, talking with one another. Sister Kenny stood at the lectern for a few minutes, waiting for the students to stand up, and when they did not, left with her entourage without giving her lecture."

In the early summer of 1943, after receiving her Bachelor of Science degree in dietetics from the University of Nebraska, Marian moved to Minneapolis to intern at UM University Hospital. She and LFP were married in November of that same year, LFP's third year of medical school. "We had no wedding cake because at the time we were married, I had been living in a dormitory and Marian was living in the nurses' residence. We had no ration coupons for sugar and butter to give the baker. There were only thirteen people at our wedding, because it was difficult to travel during wartime. We received few presents, and it was almost impossible to buy even simple appliances during the war. My mother found an old iron and a toaster in the attic, and Marian's mother donated a few pots and pans. We were married on the Saturday of a Thanksgiving weekend, and both of us went back to work on Monday. Marian continued to work as a staff dietitian in the university hospital until our son, George, was born in December 1945."

During the spring of 1944 a decision had to be made regarding further training after medical school. In those days, a match system for placing interns and residents did not exist. In order to increase the supply of physicians, the government had mandated that medical school curricula be adjusted so that students could complete their education in approximately three years, instead of the usual four. This was accomplished by changing the schedule so that the students no longer had summers free. They moved from one nine-month academic year directly into the next. Internships were limited to nine months, and those in the ASTP entered the military immediately after internship. "Because of the accelerated schedule of the medical school curriculum in place during the war, I graduated from medical school in August 1944, rather than in June 1945. Internships were to start on October 1. Money was short and travel difficult. My family advisors felt I should stay in Minneapolis if at all possible, because I had a wife, an apartment, and would soon have a baby.

"Traditionally, there had been a combined medicine-surgery internship at the university. However, this had been changed the previous year to either straight internal medicine or surgery internships. I met with the chief of medicine and inquired about the possibility of getting an internship in internal medicine. He told me that although I had finished thirty-third in a class of 130 students, he had applications from students with much higher rankings.

"I then approached Dr. Wangensteen about doing a surgical internship. The surgery department was not very popular at that time with the medical students, because the students much preferred the structured teaching that was offered in the medicine department. For example, in internal medicine the students were given booklets that contained all they needed to know for examination purposes. In the surgery department the students were advised to go to the library and look up pertinent articles. The emphasis on teaching in the surgery department was primarily designed for the residents, rather than the medical students, and many medical students floundered on the surgical services. [Additionally, it was widely appreciated that the surgical training program was very physically demanding, and it would take several years to complete.] Considering all of this, Dr. Wangensteen was surprised that a University of Minnesota medical student was interested in a surgical internship, and he agreed to take me on the spot!"

LFP noted that the surgery department's philosophy and approach to education, based on OHW's conviction that students needed to seek out information rather than being spoon-fed, continued, although not without controversy. "Later, when I became a staff member in the Department of Surgery, I recall a staff conference devoted to the teaching of medical students. After hearing all of the students' complaints, one of [my fellow] faculty members addressed OHW: 'Dr. Wangensteen, why doesn't the department hire a teacher?'"

When LFP began his internship in October 1944, everyone worked long hours. Because of the war there was a shortage of residents, and the number of interns had been reduced. "Instead of the usual eighteen interns, there were only six of us on the surgical service. First call, every third night, meant staying up all night; second call meant keeping busy until midnight, while third call meant that you might get to go home at 9:00 p.m. When I was a junior resident on Dr. Wangensteen's service the following year, I was on first call for six months. It was an invaluable experience because I operated with 'the chief' several times a week and made rounds with him daily. In this way I developed a close relationship with him. These years were hard, but everyone was stressed by the war.

"There were no hospital pagers or beepers until the 1970s. The hospital telephone operators ran the PBX boards [private branch exchange, private telephone switchboard] near the entrance to the hospital. In the morning you passed the switchboard to greet the telephone operators so they knew you were in the building. In the evening you greeted them again as you left. The operators knew all about the doctors, their wives, their habits, and their mistresses, and how to locate the doctors if they were not at home."

Halfway through LFP's internship, it was decided that one intern would be selected to stay on for an additional nine months before going into the military, and he was the one selected from his group of six. This enabled him to complete a combined eighteen months of internship and surgical residency before entering the army.

In March 1946 LFP was called to active duty and sent to Fort Sam Houston in San Antonio, Texas, for basic training. After a month of basic training he was sent to Bayreuth, Germany, where he joined the staff of the 120th Station Hospital. The hospital unit had been through

First Lieutenant Leonard F. Peltier, M.D., U.S. Army Medical Corps
1946
∾
Photo courtesy of the Peltier family

North Africa, Italy, and Southern France before arriving outside of the Winifred Wagnerheim, a 1,200-bed hospital in Bayreuth. The army hospital personnel moved in, and all of the German patients and doctors were removed, but the German nurses and technicians were retained. The hospital building was divided into two parts: one for army patients and one for the hospital personnel who used it as living quarters.

"When I arrived, the army hospital had a complete and experienced staff. Within three months most of the staff had been sent home and discharged from the service. I found myself designated as the chief of surgery of what was then a 500-bed hospital. We did no major elective operations, but we had a lot of trauma, and that is when I became interested in the treatment of injuries. While making rounds in the local [community] hospital, I also saw many cases of malnutrition in German prisoners of war returning from Russia.

"Marian and little George [not yet two years old] joined me after eighteen months. They were some of the first American dependents allowed to come to the European Theater. As the number of wives and children increased, an obstetrics-gynecology and pediatric section was added to the hospital. While in Germany, I had the opportunity to visit Prague, Vienna, Salzburg, and other cities."

LFP was discharged from the army in August 1948 and returned to Minneapolis to continue his residency training. As physicians were released from military service and returned home, competition to secure a residency position increased markedly. It had been generally agreed, however, that although there were no written contracts, the programs had a moral obligation to find places for returning veterans.

"When I returned to Minneapolis and resumed my surgical residency, I had managed a lot of trauma in the army and had become interested in the treatment of fractures. The other surgical residents were interested in stomach, gall bladder, and colon cases. Because of this, I ended up running the general surgical fracture service, using the orthopedic staff as consultants. However, as a general surgery resident I continued to do thoracoplasties, amputations, removed gall bladders and colons, resected stomachs, and removed thyroids. I also did mastectomies and some head and neck cancer operations."

During their training program, the more senior residents helped to instruct the junior residents and interns. J. Bradley Aust, M.D., Ph.D., recalled, "I first came to know Dr. Peltier when I was an intern at the University of Minnesota on one of my early surgical service assignments, and he was one of the mid-level residents. We got along quite well, and he helped to teach me to do a number of general surgical operations, most notably, for my subsequent career, a radical mastectomy. We became close friends."[13]

LFP recalled: "As residents, we worked long hours and rarely took vacations. Today, residents with wives who work can afford vacations. During my residency, vacations were virtually impossible. One of my fellow residents, Dr. Claude Hitchcock, did take a vacation. During his absence, Dr. Wangensteen would inquire 'Where is Dr. Hitchcock?' which quickly became a joke. Although Dr. Hitchcock's vacation did not imperil his residency, the rest of us were sufficiently intimidated by Dr. Wangensteen's roll call that we did not attempt to follow his example."

The surgical residency program at the University of Minnesota was not a "cookie cutter" operation. OHW believed firmly that attempting to "cover the waterfront" was futile, because the knowledge base of clinical disciplines was becoming so broad that no one could teach or absorb it all. Rather, he encouraged the residents to be able to "separate the wheat from the chaff" by familiarizing them with the origins of contemporary thought. He tried to create an atmosphere friendly to learning, to recognize the variety of talent and ability among his residents, and to encourage those of particular promise. Thus, the individual training experience of the residents varied, and the program was not attractive to those seeking the security of a regimented system. It did, however, offer surgical trainees who had more self-confidence an opportunity to express their creativity, proceed at their own pace, and to test their own ideas.[14]

The Saturday morning conference was an important vehicle for carrying out the educational process in the department. In addition to the surgical faculty, there were staff physicians from pathology and radiology who discussed cases. There were often heated disagreements between the various specialties that sometimes surprised visitors accustomed to more formal conference presentations. According to OHW, "The clinical conference in which students, house officers and faculty participate, is probably the best teaching experience in our medical schools today. We need to make the clinical-pathological conference…less of a guessing game and more of a critical review directed at ascertaining whether the therapeutic course prescribed and followed was the best that could have been offered the patient…It must be heartening to undergraduate medical students to see how fallible their professors are. It must be even more reassuring to them to hear their teachers confess their errors, pointing out how at various stages in the illness a more astute and sensitive appraisal of the situation might have had a better and happier ending."[15]

Another focus of the general surgical residency at UM was research. OHW regularly assigned one or two of the residents to work full-time in the research laboratory and continued this practice even during the war when there was a shortage of residents. He explained, "I felt strongly that the laboratory offered the best opportunity to provide the operative skills so essential in clinical surgery, and that it was the only means by which the discipline of surgery could be advanced…Students who fail to get beyond the spoon-feeding phase remain in the nursery stage of development and never attain mature growth. The student with a good appetite for knowledge soon learns that the occasional feeding by his teachers does not appease his hunger. He learns to feed himself…But the attractions of research frequently prove far more fascinating than the student had dreamed; he will stay another day to enjoy the promising prospects of the outing."[16]

Like all of the surgical residents at the University of Minnesota, LFP "spent a full year [1950-1] in the laboratory. Although Dr. Wangensteen was often criticized for sending his residents to the laboratory for an entire year, residents performed all sorts of operations on dogs and other experimental animals and emerged with good surgical techniques to apply to their patients. Dr. Wangensteen found the funding for research, and we did it. If a resident didn't have his own research ideas, the residents worked on projects of OHW, or those of other faculty members.

"My year in the research laboratory was spent working on my Ph.D. project. I obtained my Ph.D. because it was 'understood' that all of Dr. Wangensteen's successful students got a Ph.D. Usually they were in physiology under Maurice B. Visscher, M.D., Ph.D.[17] In order to get the Ph.D., you had to demonstrate proficiency in two foreign languages. German was no problem for me as I had become fluent in German during my military experience. I visited the head of the German department, we conversed in German, I translated a few pages of text, and he signed my ticket. Becoming literate in French was harder. I enrolled in a night-school class especially for students like myself. I was working full-time as a resident and missed classes when I was on call.

"The selection of my research topic was interesting.[18] I needed and received a fellowship from the National Foundation for Infantile Paralysis in 1951. Dr. Visscher suggested I study the respiratory patterns of paralyzed post-polio patients in iron lungs. I had to build and calibrate my own instrument to measure respiratory airflow, as no such instruments were commercially available. I studied eight polio patients who were confined to iron lungs, as well as six medical students who volunteered to learn to sleep in an iron lung. I even learned to sleep in the iron lung myself. Sleeping in an iron lung was not so difficult because the students and I were always tired.

"During the senior clinical year [1949-50] of my general surgery residency I was chief resident for six months. At this time I spoke to Dr. Wangensteen about my future. I didn't think there would be a place on the UM faculty for me, because there were many brilliant people in the residency program. I mentioned the possibility of going into private practice. Dr. Wangensteen responded by asking me: 'How interested could you get in orthopedics?' I replied: 'Very interested.' Dr. Wangensteen said: 'I'll talk to Dr. Cole [the chairman of orthopedics] about awarding you an orthopedic residency position. When Dr. Cole retires in four years I will make you chief of orthopedics.'"

As a result of this conversation, after LFP completed his year in the research laboratory, he spent two more years training in orthopedics (1951-3). "My position was somewhat peculiar. I served as a faculty member [Clinical Instructor in the UM Department of General Surgery] and ran the general surgical fracture service, while at the same time I was working as an orthopedic resident." This somewhat confusing situation can be explained by the fact that there were actually two fracture services at the time, one called "Trauma" or "Fractures," and a second named "Orthopedics." The "Fracture" service was staffed with general surgery residents and was part of the Department of General Surgery, while the "Orthopedic" service was a separate entity.

LFP's son, Stephen, was born in the fall of 1950 during the laboratory year of his general surgery residency. In 1951, by the time LFP was thirty-one, he had graduated from medical school, had a wife and two children, served in the army, earned a Ph.D., completed a general surgery residency, and was a UM faculty member and an orthopedic resident concurrently. At this time an incident occurred that would greatly affect LFP's future career.

"Dr. Wangensteen appeared with a foreign visitor while Dr. Cole, the chief of orthopedics, was gathered with his staff, including me in my role as orthopedic resident. Dr. Wangensteen introduced the visitor to all of the doctors present. He introduced me with the words: 'You know that Dr. Peltier is going to take over when Dr. Cole retires.' Dr. Wangensteen apparently had never discussed his plan with Dr. Cole, who had been grooming his own protégée as his successor for fifteen years. [Some of these part-time attending orthopedists] were outraged at Dr. Wangensteen's plan." Largely as a consequence of this controversy, LFP would accomplish the majority of his academic and administrative career achievements in institutions other than the University of Minnesota.

A much more immediately positive event occurred while LFP was completing his orthopedic residency. In 1952, OHW nominated him as a candidate for a prestigious Markle Scholarship. "The John and Mary R. Markle Foundation, between 1948 and 1968, supported a national program for junior medical faculty designed to identify and support young academicians with the potential of becoming the senior professors and medical leaders of the future. The selection process involved three steps: 1) the initial choice of the candidate by a committee of his medical school (each school was allowed to nominate one candidate each year); 2) selection of the finalists by a regional committee of laymen and academicians concerned with values and motivation; and 3) the final appointment of the Markle Scholars by the Board of Directors [of the Markle Foundation]."[19]

LFP explained that "competition to become the annual University of Minnesota candidate for a Markle Scholarship had become intense, and there was a lot of political infighting among the department heads. Dr. Wangensteen succeeded in having many Markle Scholars because all of his candidates were 'over-qualified.' They all had Ph.D. degrees, as well as their medical degrees. The first candidate from the university failed to make it through the selection process, but he brought back information about the system and did not fail in a later attempt.

"I competed with a few candidates from other UM departments and was selected to represent the University of Minnesota in 1952. Having been given the chance, there was a great deal of pressure to succeed. Six months before the Markle regional competition, Dr. Wangensteen made me apply for another fellowship from the National Foundation for Infantile Paralysis. I had little interest in this, because I anticipated [accurately, it turned out] that my chance to get a [second] fellowship from that Foundation was extremely poor. However, Dr. Wangensteen was very clever. He realized that whether or not I succeeded in that application process, the experience with these interviews was a great practice run for the Markle interviews.

"The annual Markle Foundation regional competition was held at the Broadmoor Hotel in Colorado Springs, Colorado. In those days travel was by train, and I went from Minneapolis to Kansas City to Denver. In Denver I met another competitor in the depot, and we took a bus tour of the area while we awaited a train to Colorado Springs.

"The competition was in the form of a continuous interview. Besides John Russell [director of the Markle selection committee] and the Markle Foundation staff, there were four older couples. Two of the men [the academicians] were the presidents of the University of Iowa and of Stanford University. One of the laymen was head of the San Francisco Community Chest, and the other was on the board of a large

Chicago hospital. The wife of the man from Chicago was a Republican Committee woman from Illinois, dedicated to Taft who was opposed for the Republican presidential nomination by Eisenhower. We spent three days with these people, sightseeing as well as enjoying lunch and dinner. We also had individual interviews. During these occasions all sorts of topics, from politics to medicine, were introduced. The political discussions at meals were very interesting. It was like walking through a minefield. Candidates were evaluated on how well they handled themselves in these situations.

"The first day, as we reported to the master suite at 9:00 a.m. for introductions, a bartender asked for our orders. Several of the candidates lost it right there. They retreated into an alcoholic haze that lasted the entire three days. Dr. Wangensteen had given me his 'Come home with your shield, or on it' speech before I left, and fortunately I came home with my shield.

"Several of the candidates whom I met at that meeting became friends for life. It was an experience that I shall never forget. Being a Markle Scholar probably affected my recruitment to the University of Kansas, where the dean, W. Clarke Wescoe, M.D., was a Markle Scholar. Later in my career I was recruited by another Markle Scholar, Merlin K. 'Monty' DuVal, M.D., at the University of Arizona. For many years a list of Markle Scholars was used by deans to identify potential recruits for their academic programs. I have been to the Broadmoor several times since to attend various meetings, and as you can imagine, it is one of my favorite hotels. That year twenty Markle Scholars were selected from eighty candidates. Each scholar received a grant of $30,000 [to be used] over a period of five years to conduct medical research. The scholars were invited to New York to meet the members of the Board of Directors of the Markle Foundation. I sat next to Junius S. Morgan (nephew of J.P. Morgan) at the dinner."

When LFP completed his orthopedic residency in 1953, he was appointed Clinical Assistant Professor in the UM Department of Surgery, Division of Orthopedic Surgery, a position he continued until 1956. During this time, in addition to his clinical activities, he was busy in his research laboratory. With the support of the Markle Scholar funding, he was pursuing his study of fat embolism,[20] a phenomenon rejected by most orthopedic surgeons at that time. Additionally, he was studying for board certification exams in general surgery and in orthopedic surgery.

"I had taken and passed the examinations for the American Board of Surgery in 1954. As I prepared to take the examinations for the American Board of Orthopaedic Surgery, the orthopedic community in Minnesota mounted a strong effort to prevent me from taking them. Someone talked to Dr. Sam Banks, the chairman of the orthopedic board committee, and told him that I had treated private patients while I was a resident, which was a breach of the rules and could disqualify me from taking the exams. This issue surfaced when I was giving a paper at the Surgical Forum[21] of the American College of Surgeons in Chicago. After the meeting Dr. Banks approached me and asked me to send him an official letter stating that I had never treated private patients while I was a resident. When I returned to Minneapolis, I spoke immediately to Dr. Wangensteen about this problem. He told me that he would intervene.

"Dr. Wangensteen then wrote a letter to Dr. Banks in which he stated that the orthopedic staff had hired orthopedic residents to treat their patients when they were on vacations and on holidays, and that he had 'tolerated this practice until now.' He then obliquely threatened to blow the whistle on the whole orthopedic residency program if they blew the whistle on me. Clearly, Dr. Wangensteen was a master of the steel-hand-in-a-velvet-glove technique and knew how to use power. As a result of this action, I was allowed to proceed with my orthopedic board examination. When I finally took the oral portion of the boards, the examiners, when I introduced myself, all remarked, 'Oh! So you're Dr. Peltier.' It was obvious that they knew the story."[22]

OHW had supreme confidence in the capabilities of his young associate, whom he described as "a very good man,"[23] and he persisted in his plan for LFP to become the head of orthopedics at UM. On 1 July 1956 LFP was promoted to Associate Professor and named by OHW as Acting Director of the Division of Orthopedic Surgery when Dr. Cole retired, even though the private orthopedic community was not happy with the appointment.

According to Dr. Aust, "In 1956, upon the retirement of Dr. Cole, the head of orthopedic surgery, Dr. Wangensteen tried to prevail in his decision to have Dr. Peltier take over as head of the Division of Orthopedic Surgery. Dr. Peltier's standing with the orthopaedic community was not at a high level, since he was viewed as primarily a general surgeon interloping into their area of expertise."[24]

LFP elaborated: "Dr. Wangensteen appointed me as Acting Head of the Division of Orthopedic Surgery when Dr. Cole retired. There was an immediate outcry from the Minnesota orthopedists who felt that Dr. Wangensteen was cramming a general surgeon down their throats. Dr. Ralph Ghormley of the Mayo Clinic called the Dean of the UM Medical School to oppose the appointment. The atmosphere was very hostile. While I controlled the university program, I did not control the program at Gillette State Hospital for Crippled Children or the Shriners Hospital, and these were essential for a complete residency [training] program."

Unbeknownst to OHW, at the time this controversy was occurring, LFP was being recruited as Professor and Chairman of the Section of Orthopedic Surgery at the University of Kansas.[25] LFP informed OHW in late August of 1956 that he was accepting the position at Kansas, to be effective on 1 January 1957.

LFP was extremely appreciative of OHW's mentoring. In his letter of resignation on 30 August 1956, LFP wrote: "It is with real regret that I leave a Medical School and Department which has nurtured and supported me throughout the difficult years of surgical apprenticeship. Any success which may come to me in the future will stem from the impetus gained from your example and the example of the many devoted students which you have gathered about you. I shall always be appreciative of the opportunities you have given me here at the University of Minnesota. I sincerely hope that you will take pleasure in knowing that a portion of the 'Minnesota leaven' is at work in Kansas and that you will watch to see how the loaves come out."[26]

OHW was extremely reluctant to accept LFP's resignation and initiated a flurry of correspondence, attempting to at least delay LFP's departure from UM until the summer of 1957, rather than in December

1956. In an attempt to dissuade LFP, on 4 September 1956, OHW contacted Frank H. Allbritten, M.D., Chairman of the Department of Surgery at the University of Kansas, explaining that UM had "put all our orthopedic eggs in one basket – in Dr. Peltier's basket, in fact," and "it is going to be impossible for us to release him by December 31, 1956."[27] On the same date, OHW wrote a similar letter to LFP.[28]

LFP, however, was firm in his decision to leave Minnesota on 31 December 1956 and assume the chair at Kansas on 1 January 1957.[29] But OHW was not willing to honor LFP's determination and wrote to him, saying "You obviously failed to read my letter [of Sept. 4] carefully. In the light of its content, I do not believe that you will want to leave here until such a time as we have our own situation reasonably resolved. This is, I feel, a very reasonable request and one with which any gentlemen [sic] would comply."[30]

Eventually, OHW resigned himself to the reality that LFP was moving on and wrote him a kind and friendly letter shortly before the Christmas holidays in 1956. "My colleagues and I regret that you will be leaving us. We can only wish you well and continuing good luck in your new environment. Let us hear from you once in awhile. Mrs. Wangensteen joins me in wishing you and your family a happy Holiday Season. With every good wish for the coming years, Sincerely, OHW."[31]

Notes and Sources

∾

1. Stanley R. Friesen, M.D., Ph.D., Professor Emeritus of Surgery and the History and Philosophy of Medicine, University of Kansas School of Medicine, letter to JGL, October 11, 1999.

2. Leonard F. Peltier, and J. Bradley Aust, *L'Étoile du Nord: an Account of Owen Harding Wangensteen (1898-1981)* (Chicago: American College of Surgeons, 1994), p. 75. Oscar Creech, Jr., M.D., was chairman of a site visit committee reviewing Owen H. Wangensteen's program for accreditation by the American Board of Surgery. He further added in that quotation, "I urge that our committee approve his program."

3. Elliott Memorial Hospital is still standing. It was incorporated into the new hospital complex, called University Hospital, completed in 1986. The site of the new hospital is where the old nurses' residence, Powell Hall, once stood, and is adjacent to the old hospital. Powell Hall was razed in 1981. In 1997 the University Hospital was sold to Fairview Health System and was re-named Fairview-University Medical Center. (Karen Klinkenberg, University of Minnesota Archives, personal communication to FWR, December 2003).

4. Peltier and Aust, p. 8.

5. Abraham Flexner, *Medical Education in the United States and Canada*, Bulletin no. 4. (New York: Carnegie Foundation for the Advancement of Teaching, 1910). Abraham Flexner was not a doctor, but was a secondary school teacher and principal for nineteen years in Louisville, Kentucky. Flexner then took graduate work at Harvard and the University of Berlin and joined the research staff of the Carnegie Foundation for the Advancement of Teaching. His published research about medical education is known as the Flexner Report. At the time of the Report, many medical schools were proprietary schools operated more for profit than for education. In their stead, Flexner proposed medical schools in the German tradition of strong biomedical sciences together with hands-on clinical training. The Flexner Report caused many medical schools to close down and most of the remaining schools were reformed to conform to the Flexnerian model. http://www.medicinenet.com/script/main/art.asp?ArticleKey=8727&pf=3&track=qpadict

6. Peltier and Aust, p. 8.

7. Ibid., p. 30.

8. Helen Clapesattle, *The Doctors Mayo* (Rochester, MN: Mayo Foundation for Medical Education and Research, 1990), pp. 328-37.

9. Ibid.

10. Peltier and Aust, p. 8

11. Ibid., p. 11.

12. Colonel William S. Mullins, MSC, USA (editor), "Medical Training in World War II," in *Medical Department, United States Army*, http://history.amedd.army.mil/booksdocs/wwii/medtrain/default.htm

13. J. Bradley Aust, M.D., Ph.D., Professor of Surgery, Department of Surgery, University of Texas Health Science Center at San Antonio, letter to JGL, October 5, 1999.

14. Peltier and Aust, pp. 75-6.

15. Ibid.

16. Ibid., p. 72.

17. Maurice B. Visscher received Ph.D. and M.D. degrees from the University of Minnesota. He was Professor and Chairman of the Department of Physiology at UM for forty-one years, until he retired in 1968. He was active nationally and was president of the American Physiological Society in 1948-9.

18. Leonard F. Peltier, "Observations on Respiration Using a Pneumotachograph," *Dissertation Abstracts International*, Physiology 12, 2 (1951): p. 0209.

19. Peltier and Aust, p. 77.

20. Fat embolism is a serious medical condition that occurs when fat particles released from bone fractures enter the blood steam of the injured patient and cause damage throughout the body.

21. The Surgical Forum was established at the 1940 American College of Surgeons Clinical Congress and continues today. It was initiated by OHW to provide an opportunity "for young men interested in and pursuing the lifelong study of surgery to bring their researches before established surgical bodies." Peltier and Aust, p. 81.

22. Candidates at the orthopedic board examinations today are not identifiable by name to the examiners, but only by number. Candidates know who will examine them and are asked to disqualify an examiner if they know the person. Thus, the board strives for a standard of fairness based on anonymity.

23. Owen H. Wangensteen, M.D., Ph.D., Chief of the Department of Surgery, University of Minnesota Medical Center, letter to Frank F. Allbritten, Jr., M.D., Chairman, Department of Surgery, University of Kansas Medical Center, August 23, 1956.

24. Aust, letter to JGL, October 5, 1999.

25. Frank F. Allbritten, Jr., M.D., Professor of Surgery and Chairman of the Department of Surgery, University of Kansas Medical Center, recruitment letter to LFP, June 21, 1956.

26. LFP, resignation letter to OHW, August 30, 1956.

27. OHW, letter to Frank Allbritten, September 4, 1956.

28. OHW, letter to LFP, September 4, 1956.

29. LFP, letters to Frank Allbritten and OHW, September 6, 1956.

30. OHW, letter to LFP, September 6, 1956.

31. OHW, letter to LFP, December 19, 1956.

Selected Publications during tenure at UM

(Authors' note: Others are listed in the specific subject chapters,
e.g. Trauma, Fat Embolism)

GENERAL SURGERY:

Leonard F. Peltier, "Chronic Progressive Gangrene of the Skin," *Bulletin of the Minnesota Medical Foundation* 5 (1945): 56-67.

Fred T. Kolouch and Leonard F. Peltier, "Actinomycosis," *Staff Meeting Bulletin, Hospitals of the University of Minnesota* 16 (1945): 332-57.

Fred T. Kolouch and Leonard F. Peltier, "Actinomycosis," *Surgery* 20 (1946): 401-30. Included the report of the first case of abdominal actinomycosis with survival.

Leonard F. Peltier and Fred T. Kolouch, "Evaluation of Early Ambulation in Surgical Convalescence," *Staff Meeting Bulletin, Hospitals of the University of Minnesota* 17 (1946): 371-86.

T. H. Crawford Barclay, Leonard F. Peltier and Arnold J. Kremen, "An Analysis of 22 Neck Dissections Performed for Cancers of the Head and Neck," *Bulletin of the University of Minnesota Hospitals and Minnesota Medical Foundation* 22 (1950): 36-41.

T. H. Crawford Barclay, Leonard F. Peltier and Arnold J. Kremen, "Neck Dissections in the Treatment of Cancers of the Head and Neck," *Annals of Surgery* 134 (1951): 828-33.

Leonard F. Peltier, Louis B. Thomas, T. H. Crawford Barclay and Arnold J. Kremen, "The Incidence of Distant Metastases Among Patients Dying with Head and Neck Cancers," *Surgery* 30 (1951): 827-33.

Leonard F. Peltier, "The Search for Lymph Node Metastases in Cancer of the Rectum," *Surgery* 30 (1951): 443-7.

Leonard F. Peltier, "The Mechanics of Parenchymatous Embolism," *Surgery Gynecology and Obstetrics* 100 (1955): 612-8.

F. John Lewis and Leonard F. Peltier, "Multiple Planned Operations in a Patient with Residual Chondrosarcoma," *Cancer* 11 (1958): 624-6.

ORTHOPEDIC SURGERY:

Leonard F. Peltier, "Nail Design: An Important Safety Factor in Intramedullary Nailing," *Surgery* 28 (1950): 744-8.

Leonard F. Peltier, "Theoretical Hazards in the Treatment of Pathological Fractures by the Kuntscher Intramedullary Nail," *Surgery* 29 (1951): 466-72.

Leonard F. Peltier and Charles M. Nice, Jr., "Irradiation of Bone Lesions in the Presence of Metallic Intramedullary Fixation," *Radiology* 56 (1951): 248-50.

Leonard F. Peltier, "Further Observations Upon Intramedullary Pressures During the Fixation of Fractures by Kuntscher's Method," *Surgery* 30 (1951): 964-6.

Leonard F. Peltier, "Pathologic Fractures Due to Metastatic Bone Disease," *Minnesota Medicine* 40 (1957): 799-800.

BASIC RESEARCH:

Leonard F. Peltier, "Observations on Respiration Using a Pneumotachograph," *PhD Thesis*, The Graduate School, University of Minnesota, Minneapolis, Minnesota (1951). *Dissertation Abstracts International*, Physiology 12, 2 (1951): 0209.

Leonard F. Peltier and Maurice B. Visscher, "Effect of Attitude of Breathing Upon Tidal Volume," *Journal of Applied Physiology* 4 (1952): 901-6.

Leonard F. Peltier, "Obstructive Apnea in Artificially Hyperventilated Subjects During Sleep," *Journal of Applied Physiology* 5 (1953): 614-8.

BOOK CHAPTERS:

Leonard F. Peltier, "Hematogenous Osteomyelitis," chap. 35 in *Brennemann-McQuarrie, The Practice of Pediatrics*, ed. Irvine McQuarrie (1955).

Leonard F. Peltier, "Bone Tumors in Children," chap. 36 in *Brenneman-McQuarrie, The Practice of Pediatrics*, ed. Irvine McQuarrie (1955).

CHAPTER THREE

The University of Kansas

"Dr. Peltier initiated a program that emphasized the partnership of research with surgical training of orthopedic surgeons, a rare and unusual circumstance. Kansas is richer because of him."

— STANLEY R. FRIESEN, M.D., PH.D. [1]
PROFESSOR EMERITUS OF SURGERY AND THE
HISTORY AND PHILOSOPHY OF MEDICINE
UNIVERSITY OF KANSAS SCHOOL OF MEDICINE

"Dr. Peltier is one of the outstanding surgical educators of our era."

— J. BRADLEY AUST, M.D., PH.D. [2]
PROFESSOR OF SURGERY
DEPARTMENT OF SURGERY
UNIVERSITY OF TEXAS HEALTH SCIENCE CENTER
SAN ANTONIO

*L*FP assumed the position of Professor of Surgery (Orthopedics) and Chairman of the Section of Orthopedic Surgery at the University of Kansas Medical Center (KUMC) in Kansas City, Kansas, on 1 January 1957. When he joined the surgical faculty at Kansas, LFP was the youngest (age thirty-seven) section head in a Department of Surgery that had a long and distinguished history and consisted of a number of nationally-known general surgeons and surgical subspecialists. LFP described his thoughts on moving to Kansas from Minneapolis. "Moving to the University of Kansas Medical Center required a real leap of faith for my wife Marian and myself. The salary provided was only $3,600 per year; the remainder of my income was to come from private practice. Since the only other full-time staff man, Dr. Lynn O. Litton, had inherited Dr. James B. Weaver's[3] patients and had developed his own practice, to all intents and purposes I had to start from scratch to develop a patient base and an income without taking anything away from him. Fortunately, I was able to do this quickly."[4]

Like many similar institutions, the University of Kansas (KU) Medical School's formative years had not been without controversy and conflict. In 1895 the Kansas legislature approved a bill authorizing the university to build a hospital and provide for its operating expenses. The main KU campus is located in Lawrence, Kansas, forty miles west of the Kansas City area. However, in order to have a larger population of patients available for teaching purposes, it was decided to put the clinical (patient-care) portion (second two years) of the medical school and the hospital in Kansas City. Students in the first two years of medical

University of Kansas Medical Center
1964
∽
Photo courtesy of the University of Kansas Medical Center Archives
Department of History and Philosophy of Medicine

school obtained their basic science laboratory and classroom education on the Lawrence campus.

The location of the hospital in the Kansas City area created a tug-of-war across the state line between factions in Kansas and Missouri because the added competition of the new hospital disrupted the pattern of care provided by the existing hospitals. Finally, the controversy was resolved in 1905, and clinical instruction began at a new hospital, built on land in Rosedale, Kansas, donated by a local entrepreneur, Simeon B. Bell. This hospital was located north of the current KUMC on the side of a steep incline, dubbed "Goat Hill" because some thought that only goats could navigate it![5, 6]

Just as at the University of Minnesota, the Flexner Report,[7] published in 1910, was critical of this new KU Medical School. Criticisms included:

1. The arrangements were entirely inadequate.

2. The hospital was too small, the faculty did not see enough patients, and the faculty lacked men whose medical training had been modern.

3. The faculty spent more time in private practice rather than teaching.

4. The medical school had "several halves" with unsettled fundamental questions regarding location, organization, and general scope. A major concern was that the first half (two didactic years) of medical school instruction took place on the Lawrence campus, and the final half (two clinical years) at the Kansas City location.

In spite of the critical Flexner Report, the medical school continued to develop, and a new, larger hospital and teaching facility, the first Bell Memorial Hospital, was built in 1924, a mile south of the old "Goat Hill" facility. However, it was not until 1962 that all four years of the medical school were consolidated at this Kansas City, Kansas, site. Even then, faculty members from the basic science departments at KU were not pleased with the move from the Lawrence campus to Kansas City.

Another issue during the early years was the relationship between teaching and private practice for the clinical faculty members. This was another of the "halves" referred to in the Flexner Report: faculty who were doing half-time teaching and half-time private practice away from the KU facility. In 1950 Franklin D. Murphy, M.D., Dean of the KU School of Medicine, created a "geographic full-time plan" to solve this problem. All full-time department and section heads, and other key faculty, were provided offices at the medical center where they could see private patients.[8] A similar arrangement continues today.

When LFP arrived at KUMC, the orthopedic service consisted not only of Lynn O. Litton, M.D., but also a part-time faculty member, W. D. "Dave" Francisco, M.D., and two residents: Charles E. Workman, M.D. (KU '57), who was to finish his residency within six months, and Wallace D. Holderman, M.D. (KU '59), who had started his residency only six months previously. Dr. Litton was a native Kansan who had completed his undergraduate and medical degrees and residency at KU. He was a general orthopedist with special interests in sports medicine and scoliosis. Dr. Dave Francisco,[9] also a native Kansan who had completed his entire education at KU, had a busy private general orthopedic practice in Kansas City, Kansas. However, in 1951 at the request of Dr. Weaver, he founded a cerebral palsy clinic at KUMC and directed it for many years. Dr. Dave was not the first member of the Francisco family who contributed significantly to the orthopedic section at KU. His father, C.B. Francisco, M.D., was the first fully-trained orthopedic surgeon to practice in Kansas City and was head of the orthopedic surgery section at KU from 1909 until his death in 1944, with the exception of the two years (1917-9) that he spent overseas with the renowned Goldthwait unit in World War I.[10]

In 1957 the orthopedic section was housed, strategically, on the ground floor of the main hospital across the corridor from the emergency room (ER), which, in turn, was located one floor directly below the X-ray department. The orthopedic office and outpatient facilities consisted of a large office (shared by Drs. Litton and LFP), a smaller office occupied by the section's lone secretary, and a clinic area large enough to have six examining tables with draw curtains to provide a modicum of patient privacy. The clinic area also had a bank of X-ray viewing boxes on one wall and was large enough to handle twenty to twenty-five attendees at the 8:00 Saturday morning X-ray conferences. The cast (plaster) room, that in reality served as an overflow for less critical patients being seen and treated through the ER, was directly across the corridor from the orthopedic clinic. The cast room was large enough for general plaster work and to accommodate the Risser table used to apply body plaster jackets for treatment of scoliosis and a fracture table used to apply hip spicas for fractured femurs.

In the mid-1960s the orthopedic offices and clinic were moved to the fifth floor of a newly constructed outpatient clinic building along with the other surgical subspecialties. This new area had a large conference room with multi-paneled X-ray view boxes, a cast (plaster) room, and eight individual patient examining rooms, each with an X-ray view box.

Shortly after LFP arrived at KUMC, he encountered a controversy between the clinical faculty and the administration. "Dr. James B. Weaver, the previous chief of orthopedics, had died of a lingering illness eighteen months prior to my arrival on January 1, 1957. He was a much-beloved figure in the community and had spent the last few years of his life raising funds for a center for crippled children. Dean [W. Clarke] Wescoe[11] had made the decision that these funds should be used for a children's center under the direction of the department of pediatrics, and it would not be an orthopedic facility. When my appointment to succeed Dr. Weaver was discussed with me, one of the conditions which Wescoe insisted upon was that I not attempt to reverse this decision. Because pediatric orthopedics was not a high priority with me, I agreed. Dr. Weaver's friends and associates were upset with this agreement, and it caused a great deal of resentment and misunderstanding during the early years of my tenure."[12] As compensation for placing the crippled children's facility in the pediatric department instead of orthopedics, Dean Wescoe did provide a small amount of space and funding to establish the James B. Weaver Orthopedic Laboratory. This lab provided the section, for the first time, with research facilities in which LFP was able to continue his work on fat embolism and the use of plaster of Paris to fill defects in bone.

In 1957 the *Kansas City Star*[13] publicized the newly established lab. "The James B. Weaver Laboratory for orthopedic surgery is now in use at the University of Kansas. Equipped for clinical chemistry and research, the laboratory also contains the bank of human bone established by Dr. Weaver for use as transplants and grafts in reconstructive surgery for children and adults." The article described LFP's plans to use the laboratory in his study of fat embolism.

James B. Weaver Orthopedic Laboratory Dedication
Spring 1957

(L to R): Lynn O. Litton, M.D.; W. Clarke Wescoe, M.D., Dean, School of Medicine; Frank F. Allbritten, M.D., Head, Department of Surgery; LFP; Vernon E. Wilson, M.D., Assistant Dean, School of Medicine;[14] Mrs. James B. "Becky" Weaver

Photo courtesy of the University of Kansas Medical Center Archives
Department of History and Philosophy of Medicine

Sing-Ping Lai was LFP's first laboratory research assistant at KU. She was a significant contributor and one of his co-authors on five important fat embolism research articles that appeared within the three-year period from 1959 to 1961. (See Publications, Chapter 7, Fat

Embolism). Marian Kuenzig,[15] who replaced Sing-Ping Lai, described the laboratory facilities during her years at KU (approximately 1960-71). "The laboratory was a small one, in the hospital building that also housed the orthopedic section. In fact, the lab was almost directly opposite the room where casts were applied and removed. This was convenient for the doctors (at that time Dr. Litton was also doing a project at one end of the little space) as they only had to step down the hall from their office or across the corridor from the Cast Room to get to the lab. I liked this part of it because I had access to what was going on in the world outside the lab, but I did not like to hear the saw as the casts were being cut, and I hated to work with the door closed. I felt really cramped for space when the residents began to participate in research, as they were encouraged to do by Dr. Peltier." LFP's persistent requests and his undeniable success as a laboratory researcher were rewarded by the hospital and school administration. Ms. Kuenzig continued, "After some months I heard the announcement that we were moving to one of the science buildings across the courtyard and would be getting more space! The place we moved to, in Hixon Hall (I believe it was called), was connected to the hospital by a tunnel that crossed under the courtyard driveway, and our labs were right at the end of this tunnel. I was concerned about being cut off from everything but this did not happen. A great deal of hospital traffic went by my door all day long. By the time he left the University of Kansas, Dr. Peltier had acquired the shared use of a large room adjoining a laboratory used for chemical analyses, in addition to a large surgery lab across the hall, fully equipped with operating table, OR lights, autoclave, and a small X-ray unit. He left the Orthopedic Section well set-up and equipped to continue laboratory research." When the location of the orthopedic laboratory facility changed, the designation "James B. Weaver Laboratory" accompanied it.

Early on, the recruitment of residents to fill the vacancies in the training program was challenging, but soon improved, and the section "provided a steady stream of very-well trained young orthopedic surgeons, many of whom have settled in the area."[16] LFP was very proud of the fact that all twenty-one orthopedic residents he trained at KU obtained board certification. Three of them became full-time academicians and remained so throughout their careers. Frederick W. Reckling, M.D. (FWR) (KU '64), and Robert G. Volz, M.D. (KU '64), became full professors and heads of their Sections of Orthopedic Surgery at KU and the University of Arizona (UA), respectively. Donald P. Speer, M.D. (UA '73), who started his residency in Kansas and finished in Arizona, became a full professor and head of Pediatric Orthopedics at UA. Another KU trainee, Federico Adler, M.D. (KU '60), served as a full-time faculty member in the Section of Orthopedic Surgery at KU for a few years immediately after he completed his residency. He subsequently practiced private orthopedic surgery for many years in Kansas City, Missouri, but remained as an adjunct faculty member at KU, supervising the scoliosis clinic that he had helped to develop at KUMC. He returned to the full-time faculty at KU on 1 July 1993 at the Kansas City Veterans Administration (VA) Hospital.

Orthopedic Residents Trained by LFP while Chairman at the University of Kansas (1957 to 1971)

∾

NAME	RESIDENCY COMPLETED	NAME	RESIDENCY COMPLETED
Charles Workman, M.D. *	1957	James Laidlaw, M.D.	1969
Wallace Holderman, M.D. *	1959	Phillip Baker, M.D.	1970
W. Robert Orr, M.D.	1959	Melvin Roberts, M.D.	1970
Federico Adler, M.D.	1960	Bernard Albina, M.D.	1971
James Dinsmore, M.D.	1961	John Pazell, M.D.	1971
George Shaw, M.D.	1961	Samuel Kaplan, M.D.**	1972
Robert Finkle, M.D.	1962	James Glenn, M.D. **	1973
Frederick Reckling, M.D.	1964		
Robert Volz, M.D.	1964	* Some training obtained at KU prior to LFP's arrival at Kansas	
Donald Spencer, M.D.	1965		
Lawrence Strathman, M.D.	1966	**Some training obtained at KU prior to LFP's departure from Kansas	
James Garner, M.D.	1967		
Howard Ellfeldt, M.D.	1968		
John Wertzberger, M.D.	1968		

LFP was developing a distinctive teaching style that was appreciated, not only by his own residents, but was known throughout the hospital. His sense of humor and quick wit, combined with his in-depth knowledge of history, and his keen sense of the poignant significance of any given situation, have left a legacy of indelible memories and anecdotes. FWR remembers, in the early to mid-1960s, when orthopedic residents would call LFP from the ER with barely-suppressed anxiety in their voices after their initial evaluation of one or more severely injured patient(s), they were often met with the response, "relax, Papa's here." This happened frequently enough that LFP was referred to, fondly, as "Papa" or "Pappy," out of earshot, of course. Nearly forty years later, upon hearing of the death of LFP, one former KU resident sincerely exclaimed, "I'm so sorry to hear that 'Pappy' died!"[17]

**University of Kansas Orthopedic Surgery Staff and Residents
1968**

∞

(L to R): James Laidlaw, FWR, LFP, John Pazell, Bernard Albina, unidentified general surgery resident

Photo courtesy of FWR

Always vigilant, if tied up in the outpatient clinic while a senior resident was in the operating room (OR) dealing with an injured patient, LFP would call the OR between clinic patients to see how things were going. If the resident responded with a comment such as "It's difficult, but we are doing the best we can," LFP would reply, "Just remember, the road to hell is paved with good intentions!"

LFP's relationship with faculty members throughout the medical center was one of mutual respect, as well as shared humor. FWR recalls accompanying LFP when he was asked to evaluate a patient of Mahlon Delp, M.D., Chairman of the Department of Internal Medicine. The patient had Ehlers-Danlos syndrome, a congenital hereditary syndrome that is characterized by hyperextensibility of the joints and extreme hyperelasticity of the skin. The patient demonstrated that he could pull the skin of his forearms six inches away from the bones. Dr. Delp was a superb clinician and extremely well-read, and was widely recognized as having a serious, stern demeanor, particularly when dealing with house officers and medical students. In discussing the case, LFP mentioned that a case of Ehlers-Danlos was described in the *Bible*. Dr. Delp, a bit of a biblical scholar, skeptically asked, "Where?" LFP replied, with a twinkle in his eye, "there is a passage in the *Bible* that speaks about Balaam who tied his ass to a tree and walked for miles!"[18] The situation further deteriorated when LFP asked Dr. Delp if he knew who the second shortest man in the *Bible* was. Dr. Delp said he had no idea, whereupon LFP replied, "Nehemiah" (knee-hi-miah). Dr. Delp then commented, "I suppose you're going to tell me who the shortest was." LFP replied, "Yes, it was Bildad the Shuhite."[19] At this final comment, Dr. Delp was, uncharacteristically, barely able to contain his laughter, and turned away to hide his grin.

LFP's working relationship with nurses was respectful, friendly and sometimes humorous. For a few brief months LFP, for some unknown reason, became an incessant cigar smoker. He would puff away until there was an inch or more of ash at the cigar tip before finding an appropriate receptacle for the ashes. One day, while observing the application of a body cast in the plaster room juxtaposed to the ER, LFP was puffing away with an inch or so of ash at the tip of his cigar.

Another observer of the activity was the head ER nurse who was well respected by the medical staff, including LFP. During her career she had served in the armed forces and had considerable physical countenance. When his cigar ash had grown about as long as it could without falling off, LFP eyed the nurse's uniform pocket and reached to tap the ashes into it. The nurse immediately retorted, "If you do,

Fat Embolism Anyone?

∽

LFP and Charles Brackett, M.D. (neurosurgeon), behind the counter. It was a long-standing tradition for the attending staff physicians at KU Medical Center to serve lunch in the hospital cafeteria just before Christmas.

Photo courtesy of the University of Kansas Medical Center Archives
Department of History and Philosophy of Medicine

you'll be lying on the floor on your back in two seconds!" LFP, recognizing the veracity of the statement, grinned and replied, "I see." He immediately found a proper container for the ashes.

There were rare situations when LFP's actions or words, initially thought to be outrageous, were met with laughing disbelief by a group of residents. He would slightly flush at their response, and counter by saying, "you Philistines!" In most instances he would later be proven correct. His sense of humor and intellect was appreciated, and his excellence in teaching, research, and clinical service was recognized and rewarded by his election in 1968 to the Kansas chapter of Alpha Omega Alpha, a North American (United States and Canada) medical honorary society.

Trauma was a major interest of LFP throughout his career. One of his first steps at KUMC was to set up a weekly trauma conference that took place in one of the major teaching auditoriums at 4:00 p.m. every Monday. Even in those early years, long before the advent of a trauma subspecialty per se, LFP recognized the importance of a multidisciplinary approach to the multiply-injured patient. The format of the trauma conference involved a case presentation of a recently injured patient by a resident from one of the surgical disciplines, followed by discussion of the patient's care. The staff surgeons in the department cooperated to make the conference a success, and faculty members and residents from general surgery and the surgical subspecialties, as well as medical students and nurses, attended.

Although this was a popular teaching tool, LFP became concerned that systematic, formal case presentations of trauma care, two or three weeks after they occurred, could not accurately and completely capture the actual fast-moving ER scenario. As he explained: "Case presentation is not an effective exercise in dealing with the patient's urgent presenting problems and the medical response to them, because the sequence of events cannot be adequately portrayed at a later time, and the complex subsequent actions, interactions, and decisions of the ER team cannot be convincingly reconstructed from the records. The students normally working in the ER are frequently so concerned with the urgent details of the patient's care that effective instruction is impossible."

LFP therefore initiated an audio-visual program to produce television tapes of real-time trauma management in the ER. Audio-visual recordings were made as emergency treatment was being administered to forty-five individual patients. Tapes of eight cases were shown later during the weekly trauma conferences. When the videotapes were used instead of a case presentation as a teaching tool, they were quite successful. Attendance, attention, and relevant questions and discussions by students and staff increased with use of the tapes. The tapes also showed promise as investigative tools to study the organization and inter-personal relationships of the ER personnel, including the behavior of the team under stress. The equipment used in the ER videotaping project included a system of recording the elapsing time, as well as the activity taking place. Performing care with dispatch and avoiding delays is, of course, important in emergency care. Thus, having a record of the time frame of activities could be useful in streamlining activities and expediting care. Recordings were often made without the consent of the patients, who usually were unconscious at the time of arrival in the ER. In such cases, the tapes were erased without viewing, if the consent could not be obtained from either the patient or a legal guardian within twenty-four hours. Although this videotaping endeavor showed promise as both a teaching strategy and a valid research method, it was suppressed because of the fear of medical-legal problems.

An important facet of orthopedic surgery is the management of children with deformities and crippling disorders. In fact, the word orthopaedic, coined by Nicolas Andry[20] is derived from the Greek words *orthos*, meaning straight, and *paidion*, referring to a child. The internationally recognized symbol for orthopedics is a crooked sapling, attached to a straight wooden post by several encircling loops of rope that can be tightened as straightening occurs.

During his tenure at KUMC, LFP worked with an artist, Beverly Brewster,[21] in the medical center's design and illustration department to create a "Kansas version" of the traditional orthopedic crooked tree symbol, a crooked sunflower. Ms. Brewster recalls LFP's relationship with the KUMC design and illustration department and the events leading to creating the crooked sunflower: "Dr. Peltier came to order

The "Crooked Tree"

∾

Original illustration in Nicolas Andry's classic 1741 volume in which the word "orthopaedics" was coined.

Photo courtesy of the Jeremy Norman Publishing Company, San Francisco

drawings or graphs fairly often. As time passed, we in the studio began to get acquainted with him. Early on he'd revealed his love of reading and of rare books. Soon, it was obvious that he was captivated by the collection of medical antiquities in the History of Medicine Library. Somewhere along the way, he introduced me to a special selection in the rare books collection; the writings of the early-day Physician-Surgeons who treated young patients with crooked legs surprised me....The Nicolas Andry treatise...was new and fascinating to me. It was a revelation to learn that these medical men observed and were impressed by the successful results of Medieval Plantsmen's care of crooked sapling trees: twisted young trunks bound snugly to strong stakes were induced to grow in a straight direction. The application to the children's plight was recognized and implemented....Medical progress!!...At some point, Dr. P. asked me to help develop a not-too-serious design related to his work. The early lithographs and engravings of crooked trees presented an irresistible image....It was a simple and whimsical evolution from the Nicolas Andry piece to the resulting illustration for Dr. Peltier, the Orthopedist at Kansas University in the Sunflower State." Later, just before he moved to Arizona, LFP worked with Ms. Brewster to create a crooked saguaro cactus logo.

Children with a variety of disabilities were cared for at KUMC, many in orthopedic crippled children's clinics. Among those were children with scoliosis, cerebral palsy, and congenital spinal deformities, such as myelomeningocele. Separate clinics for cerebral palsy (a disability resulting from damage to the brain before, during, or shortly after birth and outwardly manifested by muscular incoordination, spastic paralysis, and speech disturbances), and scoliosis, (a rotatory lateral curvature of the spine), as well as a general crippled children's clinic (clubfeet, bow legs, congenital hip dysplasia, etc.), had been established prior to LFP's arrival at KU. The care of many of these children was financially supported by Easter Seals[22] and the Kansas Society for Crippled Children.

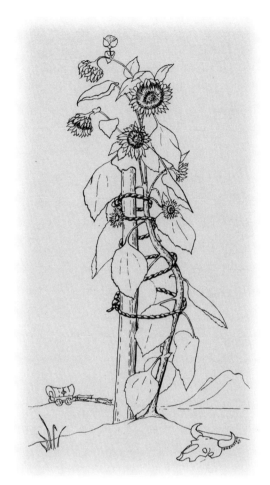

The Crooked Sunflower

∾

The crooked sunflower is an adaptation of the Nicolas Andry crooked tree, created by LFP and Beverly Brewster. Ms. Brewster explained the symbolism of the drawing: "The covered wagon with the characteristic medical vehicle symbol, the cross, represented LFP's westward trek from Minnesota, much in the spirit of our early pioneers and their migrations to the West in search of new opportunities. 'Onward and Upward!' The oxen skull was LFP's rueful acknowledgment of the reality that we all will, someday, be bones, quietly returning to the elements."

Original drawing by Beverly Brewster
Courtesy of the Peltier family

The cerebral palsy clinic founded by Dr. Dave Francisco had provided, from its inception, multispecialty care, with a neurologist, speech pathologist, physical therapists, occupational therapists, and other specialists as needed. Dr. Litton, with the assistance of Dr. Adler, had started a scoliosis clinic. Special equipment and operating instruments necessary for the care of these patients were obtained. An orthotist, Wallace Whitney, became an expert in making individually-fitted "Milwaukee" braces and other orthotic devices to treat spinal curvatures.

Some of the most challenging pediatric patients, and their parents as well, were those children with myelomeningocele (protrusion of the spinal cord and its meninges, or covering, through a defect in the vertebral canal). This congenital spinal defect often resulted in paralysis, with loss of both sensory (feeling) and motor (movement) nerve function in the lower extremities and loss of bladder and bowel control. Not only did these children need to be seen by the orthopedist, but also by the urologist and the neurosurgeon in separate, often uncoordinated clinics. To rectify this, with the cooperation of urology and neurosurgery faculty members, LFP initiated a special "one-stop" clinic for these patients. Professionals from various rehabilitation disciplines, such as hearing, child psychology, physical therapy, and social services also participated. At this clinic, considered a great improvement by everyone, the patients and their families could be seen by all of the various specialists at the same time and in the same place.

Because of the success of this clinic, the Kansas Society for Crippled Children provided funds for Donald L. Rose, M.D. (rehabilitation), Charles E. Brackett, Jr., M.D. (neurosurgery), and LFP to attend an international meeting during the late 1960s in the Netherlands devoted to myelomeningocele. Prior to this meeting the group toured national centers for crippled children in the British Isles. LFP remembered: "During our trip to Europe we spent two weeks visiting hospitals in London, Sheffield, and Edinburgh and discovered that their programs were much the same as ours. At the hospitals for crippled children in England we saw a lot of thalidomide cases [children with missing limbs due to a medication their mothers had taken during pregnancy]. We also attended an international conference in The Hague, where we met [professional] people from all over the world."[23]

Long before the emergence of sports medicine as an orthopedic subspecialty, and the advent of arthroscopy and complex surgical reconstructive procedures, LFP and Dr. Litton initiated and conducted an annual educational program for coaches involved with children's athletic activities in the Kansas City area. They co-authored a book in 1963 entitled *Athletic Injuries*[24] (LFP's first published book).

Educating coaches in methods of recognition and prevention of athletic injuries was vital in preventing life-long severe and permanent deformities. In children at the elementary and middle school levels, one of the most serious and fairly common injuries is to a growth center (epiphyseal plate) of an extremity. If injuries of this type are not prevented or recognized and appropriately treated, disturbances of growth can occur, leaving a child with a short and/or deformed arm or leg. Unlike the multi-volume sports medicine textbooks of today, this small book, with its simplistic but clear diagrams, describes the fundamentals of the anatomy and injuries in basic terms, making it useful for lay persons as well as family practitioners who may be the first to encounter these patients.

"After working with me for almost ten years, Dr.

Litton & Peltier, *Athletic Injuries*, 1963

ᜫ

Courtesy of Federico Adler, M.D., Photo courtesy of the University of Kansas Medical Center Archives, Department of History and Philosophy of Medicine

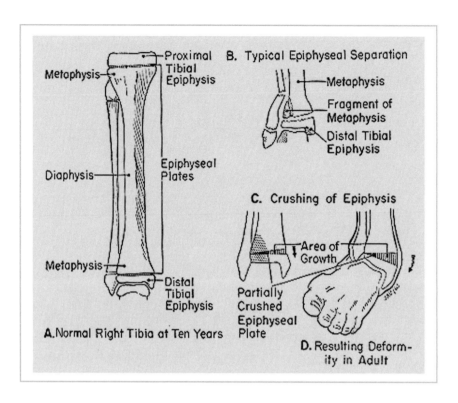

Consequence of Injury to the Growth Centers:
Potential Permanent Deformities in Childhood and Adolescence

∽

Lynn O. Litton and Leonard F. Peltier, "Athletic Injuries,"
(Boston: Little, Brown, & Co., 1963), p.27; used with permission
of Lippincott, Williams & Wilkins©

Litton became chief of orthopedics at the University of Missouri College of Medicine in Columbia, Missouri. His departure left me almost alone at the helm of a very busy orthopedic service. In July of 1966 I was able to recruit Dr. Fred Reckling to fill Dr. Litton's position. Dr. Reckling had completed his orthopedic residency at KUMC in 1964 and spent two years as an orthopedic surgeon in the United States Air Force. His arrival stabilized the orthopedic service and its teaching program."[25]

"The University of Kansas, the Kansas University Medical Center, and the Kansas City community were very good to me and to my family. Our boys were eleven and six when we arrived. Our oldest son, George, received his medical degree from the University of Kansas Medical School and also postgraduate training in general surgery and plastic surgery. Our son, Stephen, received his bachelor's degree from the University of Kansas. [After attending summer school at KUMC to update her licensure from the American Dietetic Association, Marian Peltier worked in the Diet Kitchen for the Clinical Research Unit at KUMC for a few years.] The collegial atmosphere in the hospital made it a pleasant and stimulating place to work. Of special importance to me was the opportunity to become acquainted with Ralph H. Major, M.D., who nurtured my continuing interest in the history of medicine."[26] LFP's love for books and eagerness to share them with colleagues and friends was done with humor, as can be seen by his personal bookplate.

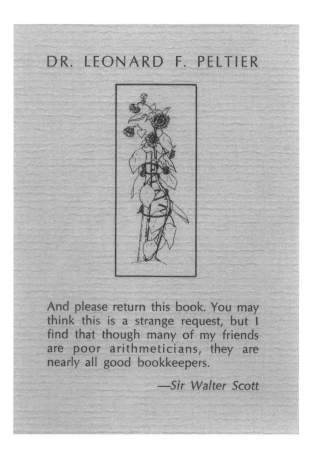

DR. LEONARD F. PELTIER

And please return this book. You may think this is a strange request, but I find that though many of my friends are poor arithmeticians, they are nearly all good bookkeepers.

—*Sir Walter Scott*

LFP's not-so-subtle bookplate

∞

Courtesy of the University of Kansas Medical Center Archives
Department of History and Philosophy of Medicine

In 1970, after almost fourteen years at KU, LFP was ready for new challenges. Things were changing at KU. The University of Arizona was in the process of opening a medical school and residency program in Tucson, and LFP was approached by Merlin K (Monty) DuVal, M.D., Dean of the new College of Medicine, and Erle E. Peacock, Jr., M.D., head of the new Department of Surgery, to join the faculty at UA as the head of the new Section of Orthopedic Surgery. LFP and Marian first visited Tucson in May 1970 to explore the possibility of accepting the position.[27]

Following that visit, LFP and Dr. Peacock carried on frequent correspondence, sharing ideas about developing an academic orthopedic surgery program. In September 1970 LFP and Marian again visited Tucson, this time with LFP spending two days in formal interviews.[28] Shortly after that visit, LFP confirmed his interest in accepting the position at UA, effective on 1 July 1971, and was welcomed with open arms by Dr. Peacock and Dr. DuVal.[29, 30]

For LFP, the opportunity proved irresistible.[31] He realized that whereas he had been the youngest section chief when he arrived at Kansas, he would be one of the founding faculty members of a new medical school at the University of Arizona, and he would have the opportunity to create his own program.[32] He was also influenced by the magnetic charm and educational philosophy of Dr. Peacock. "Erle Peacock's approach to surgical education makes me think of Dr. Wangensteen!"[33] This assessment would be challenged within three years.

Notes and Sources

1. Stanley R. Friesen, M.D., Ph.D., letter to JGL, October 11, 1999.

2. J. Bradley Aust, M.D., Ph.D., letter to JGL, October 5, 1999.

3. James B. Weaver, M.D., who began his career on the KUMC faculty in 1927, became the chief of orthopedics in 1946 and organized the orthopedic surgery residency program. He continued in his position as Chairman of the Section of Orthopedic Surgery at KU until he died in 1956.

4. Stanley R. Friesen, and Robert P. Hudson, *The Kansas School of Medicine: Eyewitness Reflections on its Formative Years* (1996), p. 264. Dr. Friesen, Professor Emeritus, Surgery and the History and Philosophy of Medicine, University of Kansas School of Medicine, obtained his A.B. and M.D. degrees from KU, and his Ph.D. from Minnesota. He was a student of OHW, as was LFP. Dr. Hudson, Professor Emeritus, History and Philosophy of Medicine, University of Kansas School of Medicine, obtained his undergraduate and M.D. degrees from KU, and his M.A. in medical history from Johns Hopkins. Both authors spent the majority of their professional lives as professors in the KU School of Medicine and were eyewitnesses to the school's formative years.

5. Ibid.

6. C. S. Griffin, *University of Kansas* (Lawrence, KS: University Press of Kansas, 1974).

7. Abraham Flexner, *Medical Education in the United States and Canada, Bulletin No. 4.* (New York: Carnegie Foundation for the Advancement of Teaching, 1910).

8. Griffin, 1974.

9. In 1985 Dr. Dave Francisco joined the university faculty full-time and supervised the program at the Kansas City Veterans Administration (VA) Hospital.

10. Leonard F. Peltier, "The Division of Orthopaedic Surgery in the A.E.F., a.k.a. The Goldthwait Unit," *Clinical Orthopaedics and Related Research* 200 (1985): 45-9. The Goldthwait Unit was a group of twenty-one volunteer American orthopedists who responded to a call from Joel

E. Goldthwait, M.D., of Boston, in 1917, to join the American Expeditionary Forces in Europe during World War I. The outstanding young orthopedists in this group, upon returning to civilian life, had an enormous effect upon the growth and development of orthopedic surgery in the United States. They became leaders in the field, transforming the image of the orthopedist from a "strap and buckle" doctor to an orthopedic surgeon willing and able to apply surgical skills and techniques in the treatment of disabling diseases and injuries.

11. W. Clarke Wescoe, M.D., Professor of Pharmacology and Experimental Medicine, and Markle Scholar in 1949, was appointed Dean of the KU School of Medicine in 1952. He continued in this position for eight years, until he was appointed Chancellor of the University of Kansas.

12. Friesen and Hudson, 1996, p. 264.

13. "Tribute in Laboratory," *Kansas City Star*, October 6, 1957.

14. According to Friesen and Hudson, p. 19, Vernon E. Wilson, M.D., was referred to with affection and admiration by Dean Wescoe as the "grey eagle." Wilson left KU in 1959 to become Dean at the University of Missouri Medical School, Columbia. He subsequently served from 1970-2 as an administrator in the U.S. Department of Health, Education, and Welfare, and from 1974-81 as Vice President of Medical Affairs at Vanderbilt University.

15. Marian Kuenzig, letter to JGL, October 29, 1999. Marian was LFP's lab technician at the University of Kansas from approximately 1960 to 1971.

16. W. David Francisco, *A History of Orthopedic Surgery at the University of Kansas Medical Center*, Unpublished Monograph, (Kansas City: Section of Orthopedic Surgery, University of Kansas Medical Center, November 1991), p. 14.

17. Howard Ellfeldt, M.D. (KU '68), personal communication with FWR, June 2003.

18. Balaam, a prophet described in the Old Testament, was summoned by the Moabite king Balak to curse the Israelites. However, Balaam was rebuked by his ass, who refused to accompany him on the evil excursion, and he concluded his mission by blessing, instead of cursing, the Israelites. *The Bible*, Numbers 22-24.

19. Bildad the Shuhite was a contemporary of Job. *The Bible*, Job 2:11.

20. R. Kohler, "Nicholas Andry. Lyon 1658 – Paris 1742, the Grandfather of Orthopaedics," *European Orthopaedics Bulletin*, No. 2 (May 1995) http://www.diavlos.gr/orto96/ortowww/andry1.htm

21. Beverly Brewster Sherrell, former Art Director, Section of Design and Illustration, Department of Learning Resources, University of Kansas Medical Center, letter to FWR, August 28, 2003. Beverly, who later married Roy Sherrell, requested that she be referred to as Beverly

Brewster in reference to the orthopedic logo drawings as a way of honoring her first husband who was an internal medicine resident when he died in a polio epidemic in the 1950s.

22. "The Story of Easter Seals," http://www.easter-seals.org Easter Seals, a national volunteer organization whose logo is the lily, a symbol of spring, resurrection, and new life, assists more than one million children and adults with disabilities through more than 450 service sites. It also advocates for passage of legislation to help people with disabilities achieve independence.

23. Friesen and Hudson, p. 265.

24. Lynn O. Litton and Leonard F. Peltier, *Athletic Injuries* (Boston: Little Brown and Co., 1963).

25. Friesen and Hudson, p. 265.

26. Ibid., p. 266. Ralph H. Major, M.D., was a long-time Professor and Chairman of the Department of Internal Medicine at KUMC, as well as Chairman of the Department of History of Medicine.

27. Erle E. Peacock, Jr., M.D., Head of the Department of Surgery, University of Arizona College of Medicine, letter to LFP, April 29, 1970.

28. Itinerary for LFP's visit to UA, September 22 – 4, 1970.

29. Erle Peacock, letter to LFP, September 28, 1970.

30. Merlin K. DuVal, M.D., Dean, University of Arizona College of Medicine, letter to LFP, September 29, 1970.

31. Aust, letter to JGL, October 5, 1999.

32. LFP sent a written proposal for an orthopedic residency program ... "it is a viable proposal and could work for me or for someone else," to Erle Peacock, June 15, 1970.

33. LFP, personal communication with FWR, Spring, 1971.

Selected Publications during tenure at KU

(Authors' note: Others are listed in the specific subject chapters,
e.g. Trauma, Fat Embolism)

Leonard F. Peltier, "The Transmission of Sound by the Femur," *GP* 109 (January 1958).

Leonard F. Peltier, "Orthopedics," Chapter in *Brennemann- McQuarrie, The Practice of Pediatrics*, ed. Irvine McQuarrie (1958).

Leonard F. Peltier, "Examination of the Back and Extremities," chap.14 in *Major's Physical Diagnosis*, ed. Ralph H. Major and Mahlon H. Delp, 6th ed. (Philadelphia and London: W. B. Saunders Co., 1962).

Robert G. Volz and Leonard F. Peltier, "Experimental Production of Villonodular Synovitis in Rabbits," *Surgical Forum* 14 (1963): 452-3.

Robert G. Volz, Donald L. Rose and Leonard F. Peltier, "An Active Program of Treatment for Patients with Fractures of the Dorsolumbar Spine," *Surgery, Gynecology and Obstetrics* 117 (1963): 763-6.

Wallace H. Cole and Leonard F. Peltier, "Treatment of Pathologic Fractures Associated with Primary and Secondary Tumors," chap. 2 in *Treatment of Cancer and Allied Diseases*, ed. George T. Pack and Irving M. Ariel, 2nd ed., vol. VIII (New York, Evanston and London: Harper and Rowe Publishers, 1964).

Andres Grisolia and Leonard F. Peltier, "The Treatment of Fractures Complicated by the Use of Skin Grafts and Etheron Prosthetic Sponge," *Journal of Trauma* 4 (1964): 682-6.

Donald M. Spencer and Leonard F. Peltier, "Deformities Produced by Operations on the Rabbit Fetus," *Surgical Forum* 15 (1964): 441-2.

Thomas M. Holder and Leonard F. Peltier, "Symphysiotomy for Exposure in Resection of Pelvic Tumors," *Surgery* 60 (1966): 819-20.

Leonard F. Peltier, "The Treatment of Chondrosarcoma," in *Progress in Clinical Cancer*, ed. Irving M. Ariel (New York, London: Grune & Stratton, 1966), 289-96.

Leonard F. Peltier, "A History of Hip Surgery," chap. 1, in *The Adult Hip*, ed. J. J. Callaghan, Aaron Rosenberg and Harry Rubash (Philadelphia: Lippincott-Raven Publishers, 1967).

Leonard F. Peltier, "Examination of the Back and Extremities," chap. 14 in *Major's Physical Diagnosis*, ed. Ralph H. Major and Mahlon H. Delp, 7th ed. (Philadelphia and London: W. B. Saunders Co., 1968).

Leonard F. Peltier, "Radical Local Excision in the Treatment of Malignant Tumors of the Shoulder Girdle (The Tikhov-Linberg Operation): Report of a Case," *Journal of Surgical Oncology* 4 (1972): 376-9.

Leonard F. Peltier, "Examination of the Back and Extremities," chap. 14 in *Major's Physical Diagnosis*, ed. Mahlon H. Delp and Robert T. Manning (Philadelphia, London, Toronto: W. B. Saunders, Co., 1975).

CHAPTER FOUR

The University of Arizona

"Leonard Peltier is responsible for establishing and developing a strong Section of Orthopedic Surgery. His efforts during his 20 years in the College of Medicine have had a major impact in the areas of faculty recruitment and orthopedic residency training."

— JAMES E. DALEN, M.D.[1]
VICE PROVOST FOR MEDICAL AFFAIRS
DEAN, COLLEGE OF MEDICINE
UNIVERSITY OF ARIZONA MEDICAL COLLEGE

*L*FP assumed the position of Chief, Section of Orthopedic Surgery, Department of Surgery, University of Arizona (UA) College of Medicine, on 1 July 1971. He was among the first clinical faculty members hired at this "start-up" medical school, initiated more than eighty years after the 1886 inception of its parent university. It was one of fifteen new medical schools created in the United States between 1963 and 1978 as a result of federal pressure to increase the numbers of doctors.[2]

The University of Arizona itself had begun in a climate of political infighting in the 13th Territorial Legislature in 1885, twenty-seven years before Arizona became a state.[3] Cities and counties in the territory needed money because federal army revenue was ending with the conclusion of the Apache Indian wars, and the legislature controlled the purse strings. Major decisions were being made about the location of buildings and institutions that could produce income in the future. "The two big 'plums' were considered to be the capitol and the asylum for the insane [based primarily on current or potential financial rewards].

The Crooked Cactus

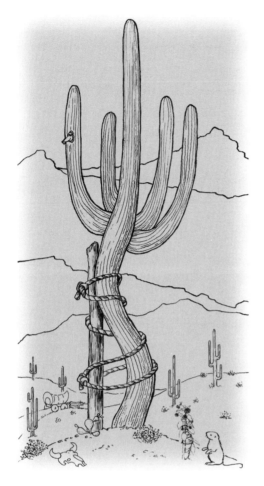

Before LFP left Kansas for Arizona, he again enlisted the creativity of Beverly Brewster, who had designed the crooked sunflower, to develop a logo for the orthopedic section at the University of Arizona. They retained the covered wagon and oxen skull and reduced the size of the crooked sunflower but kept it to indicate where the orthopedic service at Arizona got its roots.* They added a gopher to represent Minnesota, as well as mountains and arid desert landscape to represent Arizona. As a bit of humor, they inserted a Kansas Jayhawk (a mythical bird, the mascot of the University of Kansas) high in a hole in the large central saguaro, the usual habitat of the cactus wren (the Arizona state bird).

* LFP, July 4, 2000, letter to Sue Ellen Fest, secretary in UA Department of Orthopædics.

Design by Beverly Brewster
Photo courtesy of the University of Arizona Department of Orthopædic Surgery Archives

A university and a teacher's college were also to be discussed, but no one really [was interested in] them...at this point there weren't even any high schools in the territory."[4] The funds allocated for the university, $25,000, were only a fourth of the amount designated for the insane asylum. Funds designated for the Teachers College were even less: $5,000. And of course, the territorial capitol was expected to generate greater revenue over the long-term future than any of the other facilities.

Therefore, the Tucson representative, C. C. Stephens, was sent to the legislature with instructions to bring the territorial capitol back to Tucson from Prescott. Unfortunately for Mr. Stephens, the legislature decided that the territorial capitol would remain in Prescott[5] and Phoenix was awarded the insane asylum. Tucson received the university and Tempe, the Teachers College.[6] Furthermore, the appropriation for the university included the stipulation that within a year the people of Pima County must donate forty acres for its location, or the funds would lapse. When the hapless legislator returned to Tucson, hoping his good news would be welcomed, he was bitterly criticized by the local newspapers and the populace for his failure. So unpopular was the university that no one in Tucson would offer land for the project. It was not until 1886 that three local businessmen (two gamblers and a saloon-keeper, according to legend) agreed to donate forty acres of desert, and in 1887 ground was broken for the first university building.[7]

Many years later, the College of Medicine's establishment paralleled the acrimonious beginning of UA. A far-sighted UA president, Richard A. Harvill (1951-71), realized that the addition of a medical school would be a significant step in the evolution of the 20,000-student UA as a major university. When plans were undertaken to develop a medical school in Tucson, the old political contest between Phoenix and Tucson re-emerged. A blue-ribbon committee was appointed to study whether the medical school should be located in Phoenix or Tucson. Finally, after a passionate and bitter battle between UA and Arizona State University (ASU, located in the Phoenix area), the Arizona Board of Regents in 1961 authorized the establishment of the College of Medicine at UA in Tucson. The decision was based, in part, upon the premise that UA had a stronger basic sciences program than ASU.

Merlin K. "Monty" DuVal, M.D., was recruited from the University of Oklahoma by President Harvill and appointed dean of the new medical school. DuVal, a relatively young man of forty-four years, approached the task of creating a new medical college with enthusiasm and vigor. After a statewide fund-raising campaign, $3,000,000 (of the $7,000,000 needed) was raised by private donations. This enabled UA to obtain two United States Public Health Service grants for building the new College of Medicine. However, the decision to place the medical school in Tucson was a source of rancor and remained a divisive factor in the legislature for several years after the inception of the medical school. Because of the discontent, President Harvill requested that Dean DuVal open the College of Medicine in September 1967, rather than the original planned date of 1968, to prevent attempts to block the opening of the medical school by political opponents in the state legislature. There were thirty-two students enrolled in the first class, twenty-six men and six women, selected from a group of 600 applicants.[8]

LFP describes his first awareness of the new enterprise in Tucson: "The first time I heard of the new medical school in Tucson was when I attended a meeting of the American Surgical Association in Boca Raton, Florida, probably in 1968. I met Monty DuVal there. He and I had known each other for some years, and I had consulted in the care of his son, who had spondylolisthesis [forward displacement of one vertebra over another] and was injured playing football. Both of us had a free afternoon, and Monty said he was going out to the College of the Atlantic [now Florida Atlantic University] to look at their library. It was state-of-the-art, with all sorts of new computer gimmicks. He was looking for ideas to incorporate in the new College of Medicine Library in Tucson."[9]

Arizona Medical Center
Tucson, AZ
1971
∾

Photo courtesy of Special Collections, University of Arizona Library,
University of Arizona Photograph Collection,
Arizona Medical Medical Center Exterior
Photography by Manley-Prim Photography, Inc., Tucson, AZ

Great attention to detail was paid in designing the initial University Hospital and College of Medicine building, which eventually would become known as the Arizona Health Sciences Center (AHSC).[10] The library was placed in the center of the building, because it was considered by the founding faculty members as the heart of the college. It was, and still is, open twenty-four hours a day, seven days a week, with the exception of Christmas and New Year's Day. Education facilities, research laboratories, and patient care areas were stacked vertically and arranged horizontally to facilitate convenience in integrating education, research and patient care activities and allow for expansion of one area without severely impacting another. Basic science departments with strong historical relationships, such as microbiology and biochemistry, were placed on the same floors to encourage strong inter-departmental relationships. Academic faculty offices were located near their clinical areas to maximize convenience and ease during the working day. Because LFP arrived in Tucson while the hospital building was still under construction, he was able to select his office space on the fourth floor. Secretarial offices were functional but not elaborate. Green walls and green Steelcase furniture, rather than the standard university gray issue, were selected by the UA interior decorator with the intent of facilitating work productivity and worker cheerfulness. Office equipment consisted only of new IBM typewriters (non-correcting) and dictaphones, predecessors of today's computers and miniature dictation equipment.

Perhaps the most unusual feature of the new hospital was the circular design of the hospital wards with the nurses' station in the hub of the circle and patient beds on the rim. This unique arrangement allowed all patients' rooms to be readily observed from the nurses' station. The University Hospital officially opened its doors on 1 September 1971.[11] Prior to its opening, the Tucson Veterans Administration (VA) Hospital served as the primary teaching hospital for the new UA College of Medicine.

Dean DuVal took great care in recruiting faculty for the new medical school. By 1970 the College of Medicine was in its third year and 130 faculty members had been hired. When the Section of

Orthopedic Surgery in the College of Medicine at UA formally began on 1 July 1971, its faculty consisted of LFP, Professor of Surgery and Head, and Donald P. Speer, M.D., who accompanied him from the University of Kansas Medical Center. Dr. Speer was a third-year resident in orthopedic surgery, but was also appointed to the faculty as an Instructor in Surgery.

Prior to the creation of the Section of Orthopedic Surgery at UA, the clinical orthopedic service at the Tucson VA Hospital had been under the supervision of two private orthopedists, Drs. Stanley S. Tanz and Jacob B. Redekop of Tucson. Dwight Lundell, M.D., a UA general surgical resident, was rotating through the VA orthopedic service at this time. When Drs. Peltier and Speer arrived in Tucson, the UA Section of Orthopedic Surgery immediately assumed responsibility for the VA orthopedic service. On 4 October 1971, just five weeks after the new University Hospital opened, representatives of the American Board of Orthopaedic Surgery and the Committee on Accreditation of the American Hospital Association, Walter A. Hoyt, M.D., and William R. MacAusland, M.D., conducted a site visit for the purpose of accrediting the new hospital's academic orthopedic program. LFP had initiated preparations for accreditation of this new program at UA by contacting the appropriate organizations the previous fall, while he was still in Kansas.[12] The site visit was especially challenging for Dr. Speer, who was combining two roles, third-year orthopedic resident and Instructor in Surgery. During the morning, in his capacity as an orthopedic resident, he met with the review team at the University Hospital and joined them for lunch with LFP. He then rushed to the VA Hospital where he spoke with the review team again, this time in his capacity as an Instructor of Surgery.[13] As a result of that site visit, the new orthopedic residency program was subsequently accredited to train one resident per year of the four-year training program.

LFP immediately engaged the new orthopedic surgery section in academic pursuits. The section's first national academic paper, "The Obstetrical Complications of Pelvic Fractures," was presented by Dr. Speer on 16 October 1971 at the American Association for the Surgery of Trauma meeting in New York City. LFP attended the inaugural meeting of the Association of Orthopaedic Chairmen[14] in Chicago on 19 November 1971. The first international visitor to the new section (29 November to 1 December 1971) was Alexander Ross, the Senior Surgical Registrar from St. Bartholomew's Hospital in London, followed shortly thereafter (3 December 1971), by the first national visitor, Mack L. Clayton, M.D., from Denver, Colorado. By the end of LFP's first year in Tucson, four papers and two exhibits had been presented at national and local medical meetings, one journal article had been published, and one major research grant renewed.[15]

The clinical work schedule was grueling. During the early years of the orthopedic program, both orthopedic faculty members (LFP and Dr. Speer) were on call every night. LFP's weekly work schedule included two outpatient clinics at the University Hospital, two outpatient clinics at the VA Hospital, one operating day at the VA Hospital, and one operating day at the University Hospital. During this time period, a large percentage of his patients at the university hospital were emergency patients suffering from trauma due to motorcycle accidents. Because of the high incidence of these patients, LFP started referring to himself as the "Honda Professor of Orthopedics."

One of LFP's goals in founding a successful academic program was to maintain an interface with the local orthopedic community. When he arrived, he was greeted warmly. A Tucson orthopedic surgeon organized a welcoming dinner, attended by almost all of the orthopedists in Arizona. LFP joined the Pima County Medical Society, and he encouraged his staff to do the same, in order to promote good "town and gown" relationships. Employing the model he had used so effectively in Kansas, he established a Saturday morning conference in which the Tucson orthopedists were encouraged to participate by bringing their own cases for presentation and discussion. He also invited them to accompany his group on ward rounds following the conference. Reciprocally, he participated in conferences at the Tucson Medical Center. He encouraged his UA residents and those of the Maricopa County Hospital training program in Phoenix to participate in, and present papers at, the annual meeting of the Arizona Chapter of the Western Orthopaedic Association (WOA). Furthermore, he timed the visits of nationally and/or internationally known orthopedists at UA to coincide with the annual Arizona chapter meetings of the WOA. This enabled the Arizona orthopedic practice community to have exposure to these visitors who often delivered the keynote address at the WOA state meetings.

Despite LFP's efforts to facilitate good relationships between the UA orthopedic faculty members and the local orthopedic community, Tucson's Square and Compass Clinic (the local crippled children's clinic) was not interested in collaborating with the new university program, and UA did not yet have a pediatric orthopedist on the faculty. An important part of any orthopedic program is the children's service, and to be an accredited program, it is necessary to have pediatric as well as adult reconstruction and treatment of fractures. Thus, LFP was challenged to create a pediatric orthopedic training experience for his residents.

Fortunately, the Arizona Crippled Children's Hospital in Tempe, initially under the direction of Warren Colton, M.D., and later Tim Lewis, M.D., had an excellent children's service and welcomed collaboration. It was integrated with the Maricopa County Hospital in Phoenix, which was at that time attempting to establish an orthopedic residency program and needed to associate with a medical school to become accredited. According to LFP, "an interesting *quid pro quo* agreement evolved. I wrote a letter as chief of orthopedics at the medical school to the accreditation board, stating that the Phoenix program was 'associated' with the medical school. In return, Dr. Colton agreed to allow us to rotate residents from the University program through the Arizona [Crippled] Children's Hospital. It proved to be an excellent rotation and training, with the exception that the residents were not too happy to be separated from their families for six months." While the residents were at the Arizona Crippled Children's Hospital, the university continued to pay their salaries, but Maricopa County provided their board and room (in reality, an 'on-call' room).

Total joint replacement surgery, which required the use of methylmethacrylate (bone cement), made its debut in the United States in the late 1960s and early 1970s. Methylmethacrylate is often used to securely fix the metal and plastic artificial joint component parts within the bone. LFP was the first orthopedic surgeon in Tucson, and one of the first in the state, to obtain Federal Drug Administration approval to use this compound. In early 1973 LFP recruited Robert G. Volz, M.D., from Denver, to develop, diversify and head the clinical and research efforts of the UA total joint replacement program. Dr. Volz had been trained by LFP at the University of Kansas, completing his orthopedic residency in 1964. He had spent time in Wrightington, England with Sir John Charnley, the innovator of total hip replacement, to learn this new procedure, and was carrying out total hip replacements on patients in Denver. While attending a meeting on joint replacement in Denver, LFP offered Dr. Volz the opportunity to join him at UA. Aware of the large number of arthritis patients living in Arizona, and having an innate interest in research, he discussed the situation with his wife Ann, and accepted LFP's offer. The move was good for the orthopedic program at UA and for Dr. Volz, who became nationally known as a total joint surgeon, laboratory investigator, and innovator.[16]

At the end of 1974, Dr. Speer completed his general orthopedic residency at UA and moved to Chicago to complete a pediatric orthopedic fellowship with Mihran O. Tachdjian, M.D. After completing his fellowship, Dr. Speer returned to UA and initiated a pediatric orthopedic service at the University Hospital in 1975.

It is notable that these achievements occurred during a three-year period of extreme instability in the UA Department of Surgery.[17] In August of 1973 Dr. DuVal, at that time Vice President for Health Sciences at the AHSC, removed Erle E. Peacock, Jr., M.D., from his administrative position as Head of the UA Department of Surgery.[18] This action was supported, and in fact, encouraged, by the president of the university, John P. Schaefer,[19] although it was strongly opposed by a number of faculty members in the Department of Surgery.[20] In the years prior to this action, according to Dr. DuVal and others, Dr. Peacock had been notified verbally and in writing that his performance as a department head was unsatisfactory due to a number of disruptive actions. Such communications were made on a very personal and confidential basis.[21] In January 1973 the national accrediting committee[22] for the medical school was critical of the operation of the surgery department and recommended that a special progress report be sought on the situation after only one year. A number of discussions took place between the administration and Dr. Peacock, but a resolution of differences was not achieved, culminating in Dean DuVal's removal of Dr. Peacock as department head in the fall of 1973.

Shortly after Dr. Peacock's removal, Douglas Lindsey, M.D., was appointed Acting Head of the Department of Surgery at UA.[23] Dr. Peacock, as well as a number of the members of the surgery department, refused to acknowledge the leadership of the acting head. On 11 February 1974, because "the affairs of the Department of Surgery were in serious disarray and …the department was rapidly approaching a crisis of potentially explosive proportions," UA President Schaefer suspended Dr. Peacock, with pay, from academic duties at the university, and informed him of the manner in which he could set in motion the available UA faculty grievance process.[24]

Dr. Peacock and others considered the administration's action as extremely heavy-handed and in violation of due process.[25] Thus, rather than availing himself of faculty grievance procedures, Dr. Peacock elected to seek a court injunction to stay this action.[26] The court ordered UA to reinstate him as department head, but with the option to relieve him of his duties pending a hearing according to university faculty rules and regulations regarding dismissal of tenured faculty members. The controversy continued for more than two years, involving a faculty grievance committee and the American Association of University Professors (AAUP), as well as attracting the interest of academic departments across the nation. Questions were asked from both administrative and faculty perspectives about the role and power any university administration ought to have in dismissing a tenured faculty member.

In Tucson the ensuing rancor and the development of surgery department factions created an extreme backlash effect that eventually polarized and isolated the Department of Surgery faculty from the other departments and threatened the very existence of the new College of Medicine. During these years, the only section in the Department of Surgery that did not lose faculty members was the Section of Orthopedic

Surgery, an accomplishment directly attributable to LFP's skilled leadership. LFP was reticent to discuss the conflict and protected his residents. Ernest Gradillas, M.D., remembers being a resident at the time. "When I was a resident the surgery department was in turmoil, but Dr. Peltier kept it from impacting at the resident level. No one knew how Dr. Peltier felt toward Dr. Peacock. Dr. Peltier never talked (bad or good) about Dr. Peacock. Dr. Peltier reminded the residents that they had more important things to do. He never let the Peacock situation become the centerpiece of the orthopedic surgery section. As a result, orthopedics was the strongest section in the surgery department."[27]

Although approached during the turmoil to be an interim leader of the Department of Surgery, LFP refused to accept this position until a new department head had been recruited. Once the new department head was hired, LFP agreed to serve as Acting Head of the Department of Surgery for three months immediately preceding the arrival of Stephen D. Wangensteen, M.D., in the fall of 1976. Believing that his role was to "maintain order and hold things together," LFP refused to move into the department head's office during this interim period.

It was an interesting turn of events when Dr. Wangensteen, the son of LFP's mentor, Owen H. Wangensteen, M.D., Ph.D., became LFP's "boss." Stephen Wangensteen had been a child during LFP's years in Minneapolis, so, although they did not know each other, LFP had been aware of him. When Stephen Wangensteen was appointed Head of the Department of Surgery, LFP smiled broadly and commented, "I've worked for the Father, now the Son, and who knows, maybe someday I'll work for the Holy Ghost."[28]

After Dr. Wangensteen's arrival, the Department of Surgery began rebuilding, and LFP assisted him in recruiting new faculty by interviewing and entertaining the candidates when they visited Tucson. New faculty members Jack Copeland, M.D., a heart surgeon, and Charles W. Putnam, M.D., a general surgeon as well as a pharmacologist, were hired, among others, to strengthen and rebuild sections that had been decimated by the departure of numerous faculty members during the years of instability.

During the 1970s and 1980s, subspecialties in orthopedic surgery grew and expanded across the United States and the world. The previous generation of orthopedic surgeons had been primarily crippled children specialists. However, once polio and tuberculosis were controlled by vaccines and antibiotics, the need for surgical procedures related to these diseases was greatly reduced. Furthermore, early diagnosis and conservative treatment decreased the need for extensive reconstructive surgical procedures of conditions such as clubfeet, scoliosis, and congenital dislocations of the hip.

While the need for reconstructive procedures in children was decreasing, orthopedic surgeons were assuming the major responsibility for treatment of fractures. General surgeons previously had considered fracture treatment as their domain, but they became more interested in vascular, heart and abdominal surgery as progress in these areas occurred. At the same time, orthopedic surgery was growing in scope and complexity, with many new and innovative instruments and techniques, such as arthroscopy, total joint replacement, spine instrumentation and knee ligamentous reconstruction. As orthopedists learned new and demanding procedures, it was impossible for one individual to gain expertise in all of them. Thus, the orthopedic subspecialties evolved. Yet the need for comprehensive care of the trauma patient continued, and LFP was instrumental in improving care of the multiply-injured patient in Tucson, as well as nationally. (See Chapter 6, Trauma, for details).

The expansion of the Section of Orthopedic Surgery at UA paralleled the international growth and expansion of the subspecialties in orthopedic surgery. During the 1970s and 1980s the UA orthopedic resident numbers were increasing, as well as the orthopedic faculty. The program started with one resident, grew to four residents (one per year), and by 1978 totaled eight residents in the four-year program.[29]

Orthopedic subspecialists were recruited as the faculty expanded. E. C. "Ted" Percy, M.D., the first of the so-called "Canadian contingent," arrived from Montreal in 1978 to develop a sports medicine program. He was quickly followed by the arrival of Robert B. Dzioba, M.D., from Toronto (back and trauma surgery), Frederick W.

Orthopedic Residents Trained by LFP
while Chairman at the University of Arizona
(1971 to 1985)

∾

Name	Residency Completed	Name	Residency Completed
Donald Speer, M.D. *	1973	Gerald Telep, M.D.	1985
Richard Laubengayer, M.D.	1974	J. Keith Braun, M.D. **	1986
Steven Cunningham, M.D.	1975	Michael Parseghian, M.D. **	1986
David Mayer, M.D.	1976	Dwight Keller, M.D. **	1987
William Fulcher, M.D.	1978	Jay Sather, M.D. **	1987
Ernest Gradillas, M.D.	1978	James Bried, M.D. **	1988
John Kloss, M.D.	1978	Heinz Hoenecke, M.D. **	1988
Joseph Nichols, M.D.	1978	Bradley Brainard, M.D. **	1989
Thomas Peters, M.D.	1979	Francisco Valencia, M.D. **	1989
John Brugman, M.D.	1981		
Robert Karpman, M.D.	1981	* Some training at the	
Eric Fishman, M.D.	1983	University of Kansas when	
Ralph Heap, M.D.	1983	LFP was chairman there	
John Medlen, M.D.	1983	** Some training obtained	
William Quinlan, M.D.	1983	while LFP was chairman at	
James Benjamin, M.D.	1984	Arizona	
Dwite Dahms, M.D.	1984		
Leonard Mulbry, M.D.	1985		

Greenwood, M.D., from Montreal (Head of Orthopedic Surgery, VA Hospital), and J. David Gibeault, M.D., from Winnipeg (hand surgery).

Two former UA orthopedic residents, William J. Quinlan, M.D. (UA '83), (sports and trauma surgery) and James B. Benjamin, M.D. (UA '84), (total joint surgery), returned to UA as faculty members after completing advanced training in their specialties. Dr. Quinlan traveled to England to study arthroscopy and to Switzerland to study fracture management. The training program he attended in Switzerland included a comprehensive study of the physiology of bone healing as well as indications and methods of internal fixation for fracture stabilization.[30] With Dr. Volz's encouragement and facilitation, Dr. Benjamin obtained a fellowship in reconstructive orthopedic surgery at Princess Elizabeth Orthopaedic Hospital in Exeter, England, under the auspices of an internationally known total hip replacement surgeon Robin Ling.

University of Arizona Orthopedic Staff and Residents
1984-1985
(LFP's last year as Section Chair)

ॐ

FRONT ROW (L to R): Michael Pitt (radiology and orthopedics), Robert Volz,
    LFP, Anna Graham (pathology and orthopedics), Robert Dzioba
MIDDLE ROW: Donald Speer, Jay Sather, Dwight Keller, William Quinlan, James
    Benjamin, Michael Parseghian
THIRD ROW: Warren Eddy, Heinz Hoenecke, Bradley Brainard, J. Keith Braun,
    Frederick Greenwood
BACK ROW: James Bried, Gerald Telep, E. C. Percy

*Photo by Biomedical Communications Department of the College of Medicine,
University of Arizona, Courtesy of Janolyn Lo Vecchio*

The increasing numbers of orthopedic faculty and residents
required more support personnel. The first orthopedic secretary at UA
was Miss Barbara Francisco, daughter of one of LFP's colleagues in
Kansas, W. D. Francisco, M.D.[31] Virginia St. John followed Barbara,
and Janolyn Lo Vecchio joined her in 1975. By the time LFP retired in
1985 there were five people on the administrative support staff: Janolyn
Lo Vecchio, administrative assistant, and four secretaries: Susie Brandes,
Sue Ellen Fest, Joan Oldakowski, and Geraldine Schlotterer.

LFP remarked that perhaps the two most notable and innovative accomplishments of UA orthopedic faculty during these years were an artificial wrist joint (Volz total wrist arthroplasty) developed by Dr. Volz in 1973, and Dr. Speer's being honored with the John Charnley Award in 1982 for his investigative work and paper entitled "Experimental Epiphysiolysis: Etiologic Models of Slipped Capital Femoral Epiphysis."[32]

During his tenure at UA, LFP was appreciated and respected by colleagues from a variety of professional and support departments. Nurses remember his sense of humor, his respect for their input and information regarding patient care, and his willingness to teach.[33] Library and information services staff members appreciated their opportunities to work closely with him. "He is one of the true bibliophiles and medical historians I have been privileged to know."[34] "He is a renowned and careful scholar with a delightful sense of humor…a knowledgeable and conscientious library user…He will not include a reference to a book or an article unless he has had the item in his hands."[35] A cell biology professor and colleague whose native country is Czechoslovakia, Milos Chvapil, M.D., Ph.D., remembers LFP requesting assistance with the translation of a Russian text from the Crimean War. "It was written in Old Russian and I had lots of trouble with the interpretation of some terms. But Len would not quote a paper unless it was read in full!"[36]

In 1985 at age sixty-five, LFP retired as Chief of the Section of Orthopedic Surgery at the AHSC. He was succeeded by Dr. Volz. However, LFP's retirement from academic leadership was short-lived. Approximately a year later he was appointed Acting Head of the Department of Surgery, for the second time, by Dean Louis Kettel, when Dr. Stephen Wangensteen left Tucson. The problems of the Department of Surgery were quite different in 1986 than in 1976 when LFP had previously served as acting head.

LFP described this later term: "As Acting Head of the Department of Surgery in 1986, my chief goals were to maintain morale, hold things together, and to get people to work. I used a management technique of 'walking around.' I would hit the operating room at 7:00 a.m. and make a point of looking at the schedule. Then I would go to the doctor's

Changing of the Guard
1985
∾

LFP's retirement as Chair of the Section of Orthopedic Surgery at UA

Seated (L to R): Robert Volz, LFP
Standing: Frederick Greenwood, Warren Eddy, J. David Gibeault, James
Benjamin, William Quinlan, E. C. Percy, Donald Speer, Robert Dzioba

Photo courtesy of James Benjamin

dressing room and say to George Drach [Chief of the Section of Urology], or another doctor, 'It looks like you have a hard day today,' or 'It looks like you are doing an interesting case,' or a similar comment. I made a point of being visible.

"I also instituted weekly meetings of the surgical section chiefs that included the distribution of financial information and staff meeting minutes. Dr. Charles Putnam was enormously valuable. He took over the bookkeeping, utilizing a computer program that would project forwards and backwards. The result was that the rumor mill that had been booming, stopped, because there was no point in rumors if you have the correct, pertinent information."

LFP continued as Acting Head of the Department of Surgery until 1990, when he officially and permanently retired. The surgery department honored him with a retirement celebration at the La Paloma Resort in Tucson on 4 May 1990. A Leonard F. Peltier Research Award for surgical residents was established in the UA Department of Surgery. Although not accomplished during his tenure, LFP's dream for the Section of Orthopedic Surgery at UA to evolve into a Department of Orthopædic Surgery was realized on 1 July 1999. (See Preface for additional information regarding LFP's preference for the "simple" spelling of *orthopedic*, as well as the convention used by the authors throughout this biography in the use of the simple *e* versus the dipthong *æ*).

Notes and Sources

❧

1. James E. Dalen, M.D., Vice Provost for Medical Affairs; Dean, College of Medicine, University of Arizona Health Sciences Center, Retirement Brochure re: LFP, 1990.

2. Elizabeth Purcell, *Case History of Ten New Medical Schools* (New York: Josiah Macy Foundation, 1972).

3. Arizona, the 48th state, entered the union on 14 February 1912.

4. Phyllis Ball, *A Photographic History of the University of Arizona*, 2nd printing (Tucson: University of Arizona Press, 1987), p. 2. Ms. Ball graduated with a degree in English, Phi Beta Kappa and with distinction, from the University of Arizona in 1943. She was employed at the UA library for more than forty years, and compiled this history book as a special Centennial birthday present for the institution to which she had so long been devoted.

5. Prescott was designated the first territorial capitol of Arizona in 1864 because of its nearby gold fields. The territorial capitol remained in Prescott, with the exception of ten years (1867-77) when it was in Tucson, until 1889 when it was moved to Phoenix.

6. The Teachers College, founded in 1885 in Tempe as Arizona Territorial Normal School, changed its name several times as it expanded, and was designated Arizona State University in 1958.

7. Phyllis Ball, *A Photographic History of the University of Arizona*, p. 2.

8. Ibid, p. 345.

9. LFP letter to JGL, November 2, 1997.

10. When the new University Hospital opened, it shared a facility with the College of Medicine. The facility eventually became known as the Arizona Health Sciences Center as it expanded to encompass not only the College of Medicine, but also the Colleges of Nursing, Pharmacy, and Public Health, and the School of Health Professions, as well as increased numbers of patients. In the early 1980s the University Hospital became a separate financial entity from the University of Arizona, although it continues in the same geographic location and remains the primary UA teaching hospital.

11. *Orthopedic Surgery Section Activities Book 1971-1982*, University of Arizona Health Sciences Center.

12. Erle E. Peacock, Jr., M.D., letter to LFP, December 18, 1970.

13. Donald P. Speer, M.D. (UA'73), interview by JGL, 1997.

14. The Association of Orthopaedic Chairmen was organized in 1971 to provide a group who could speak with a unified voice to medical school deans about problems confronting academic departments and divisions of orthopedic surgery. In 1991 the Association changed its name to the Academic Orthopaedic Society and expanded its membership to include fellowship directors and orthopedic faculty members as well as chairmen.

15. *Orthopedic Surgery Section Activities Book 1971-1982.*

16. During his years in Tucson, Dr. Volz developed mechanical components to facilitate total joint replacement in hips, wrists, and knees. In the mid-1970s he developed a trochanteric bolt, known as the Volz bolt, for reattachment of a migrated painful trochanteric fragment that sometimes occurs after total hip replacement. During the same time period he designed a complete wrist joint replacement prosthesis. Later he was instrumental in the development of the first modular total knee replacement system referred to as the AMK (anatomic modular knee). In this system there are varying sizes of tibial polyethylene tray inserts that are selected intraoperatively to anatomically match the selected femoral metallic component, thus optimizing load transfer and reduction of potential long-term wear of the tibial polyethylene inserts.

17. Although LFP would never discuss this controversy with residents and support staff at the university, except in terms of protecting the institution, the issue is of historical importance to the academic medicine community, as well as to those who look to LFP as a role model when encountering situations of conflict and controversy. Thus, it was decided to include the information in this text, using public documents as resources.

18. Merlin K. DuVal, M.D., *Background Statement*. University of Arizona Health Sciences Center, January 23, 1974.

19. Ibid.

20. Frishauf, P. "Jousting: The University of Arizona takes on the surgeons," *New Physician*, 23, 12 (Dec. 1974): 32-9.

21. Erle E. Peacock, Jr. v. Board of Regents of the Universities and State College of Arizona, et. al., CIV 74-123 PHX-HBT, (US Dis, May 3, 1974).

22. Frishauf, (Dec. 1974): 32-9. The Association of American Medical Colleges and the American Medical Association jointly participated in the accreditation of schools of medicine through the agency of the Liaison Committee that consisted of six representatives from each of the Association's councils, two "public" members, and one representative of the federal government.

23. Ibid.

24. John P. Schaefer, President of the University of Arizona. Letter to members of the faculty, February 14, 1974.

25. Frishauf, (Dec. 1974): 32-9.

26. Peacock v. Board of Regents, 1974.

27. Ernest Gradillas, M.D. (UA '78), telephone interview with JGL, Fall 1999.

28. LFP, personal communication to FWR, 1976.

29. The length of orthopedic residency programs changed during the 1970s and 1980s. In response to a need for more specialists, the years of required training were reduced from five to four (one year of internship and three of orthopedics). However, about the same time this reduction took place, the number of residents spending a year in laboratory research increased, thus reducing the actual clinical years of orthopedic training to two. It was impossible for residents to obtain the experience needed in the increasing subspecialties during a two-year period. Thus, the training program requirement returned to a total of five years (one of internship and four orthopedic, one of which could be spent in the lab or in general surgery or other subspecialty rotations). The American Board of Orthopaedic Surgery also designates how many residents per year each program is allowed to train, based primarily on available faculty members, resources, and patient numbers and demographics.

30. The institute where he did his specialized training in Switzerland was sponsored by the AO (Association of Osteosynthesis) Foundation and ASIF (Association for the Study of Internal Fixation in Davos, Switzerland). These associations began with a group of Swiss surgeons and grew to include a number of surgeons in many countries who embraced the study of fracture healing and methods of internal fixation based on sound physiological and mechanical studies.

31. *Orthopedic Surgery Section Activities Book 1971-1982.*

32. Donald P. Speer, M.D., "Experimental Epiphysiolysis: Etiologic Models of Slipped Capital Femoral Epiphysis, " *The Hip. Proceedings of the Hip Society*. Chap. 6 (St. Louis: CV Mosby Company, December, 1982): 68-88.

33. Deborah Dodge, R.N., and Anna J. Sherlock, R.N., letters to JGL, Fall 1999, and Fall 1990, respectively.

34. Fred L. Heidenreich, Information Services, Arizona Health Sciences Library, letter to JGL, January 7, 2000.

35. Nga Nguyen, Information Services, Arizona Health Sciences Library, letter to JGL, November 15, 1999.

36. Milos Chvapil, M.D., Ph.D., Professor and Head, Retired, Section of Surgical Biology, University of Arizona College of Medicine, personal communication to FWR, November 17, 2003.

Selected Publications during tenure at UA

(Authors' note: Others are listed in the specific subject chapters, e.g. Trauma, Fat Embolism)

R. R. Simon, G. M. Stanley, H. A. Kamel and Leonard F. Peltier, "Relation of Subchondral Bone and Articular Stresses to Joint Function," *Proceedings of the Fifth International Conference on Experimental Stress Analysis*, (Undine, Italy 1974).

Robert R. Karpman, Leonard F. Peltier, C. Thies and William H. Fulcher, "Determination of Volume of Lower Extremities," *Surgical Forum* 30 (1979): 504-6.

Robert G. Volz, John G. Kloss and Leonard F. Peltier, "The Use of Methylmethacrylate as a Temporary Spacer Following En Bloc Resection of the Distal Femur," *Clinical Orthopaedics and Related Research* 147 (1980): 185-7.

M. Geczy, Leonard F. Peltier, and R. Wolbach, "Naproxen Tolerability in the Elderly: A Summary Report," *Journal of Rheumatology* 14, 2 (1987): 348-54.

CHAPTER FIVE

The Professor: The Man

"The role of the professor [of surgery] has been defined essentially as being that of teacher, surgeon, and investigator. I would suggest that two other functions of...heads of [surgical programs] should be added: sideline cheerleader and regimental water carrier."
— OWEN H. WANGENSTEEN, M.D., PH.D.[1]

"Leonard F. Peltier personifies the classic, quickly-becoming-extinct, truly academic surgeon."
— PHILIP H. KRUTZSCH, PH.D.[2]
PROFESSOR EMERITUS
DEPARTMENT OF CELL BIOLOGY AND ANATOMY
UNIVERSITY OF ARIZONA HEALTH SCIENCES CENTER

∾*T*he impact of Owen H. Wangensteen (OHW), Professor and Chairman of the Department of Surgery at the University of Minnesota, upon the career of LFP extended far beyond surgical training. LFP consciously modeled his teaching style and residency training programs after his mentor, OHW. Much like the University of Minnesota's surgical teaching program, LFP's academic orthopedic programs at the University of Kansas and the University of Arizona were not cookie cutter operations.

During his twenty-eight years as a head of a training program (1957-85), evolutionary changes occurred in the education of orthopedic surgeons. National mandates, including military service requirements, impacted residency selection procedures, educational program content, and individual resident and program evaluation processes. The number of orthopedic subspecialties mushroomed, attracting far greater numbers of medical school graduates applying for residencies.

When LFP began his career as a training chief in the mid-1950s, the selection of residents was done much more informally than later, after computerized national residency matching plans were instituted. Early on, there were no contracts, and residency positions were awarded based on a single personal interview. It was in 1965 that a resident applicant first asked LFP for a written contract.

A constant in LFP's selection of residents, in addition to their academic track record and motor skills, was his assessment of the individual applicant's character, honesty, and personal integrity. In the early years, according to LFP, "At the end of my interview, I would offer a position to the candidate, he would accept, and we would shake hands. The handshake was the contract." A formal letter of acceptance would follow.

Federico Adler, M.D., who was born in Austria and grew up in Ecuador, recalls LFP's demand for character, honesty, and personal integrity in resident selection. "LFP interviewed me in the spring of 1957 over lunch at the KU cafeteria (lunch price was 54 cents). He asked me about my plans for the future, and I told him I planned to stay and make the United States my home. Two days later I received a formal letter from him 'inviting' me to become his resident. Years later LFP asked me if I knew why he took me on. Of course, I didn't. He said, 'Because you were honest,' and he continued to say that he was aware of many foreign graduates who claimed during interviews that they planned to return to their native countries after their residencies to teach the American way there. Later he discovered almost all of them stayed in the U.S. I had told him the truth."[3]

If families accompanied the interviewees, LFP would take advantage of an opportunity to meet them. In the late-1960s when Donald P. Speer, M.D., interviewed for a residency position at the University of Kansas, Laurel Speer met LFP for the first time. Laurel related that "their first meeting took place on a sunny afternoon. It was decided since we had three children ages 6, 5, and 3, that I would sit out on the lawn and wait for them to conclude their business. I was watching the children play on the grass when I saw a man in a white coat approaching with my husband. I immediately got up, gathered the children in, and was introduced to the eminent Dr. Peltier. Our conversation was brief, pleasant, really inconsequential as these initial meetings often go. But I was both impressed and grateful that he took the time and had the interest to come down from his office and meet his future resident's family. As in every meeting between us to come, he was courtly, well spoken and kind. He never ceased to care about my husband's family, never ceased being kind and courteous to me. It is rare in the busy and high-pressure world of academic medicine that a chief of service will take the time to care about his staff's families. For Dr. Peltier, this kind of caring was natural and unstudied."[4]

When LFP first became a chairman in 1957 at the University of Kansas (KU), resident applicants were individuals from a wide range of ages and with varying experience. Many of the residency applicants were straight out of an internship, but others had extensive experience in general practice, or in the military. For example, the first resident LFP admitted to the KU program, W. Robert Orr, M.D., was forty-eight years old (approximately eleven years older than LFP) when he applied and was accepted for two years of additional residency training in orthopedic surgery at KU.[5] He had previously served an internship (Waterbury, Connecticut), a year of general surgery (Henry Ford Hospital, Detroit, Michigan), had two years of military experience after Pearl Harbor, and was a general practitioner in Mishawaka, Indiana.

However, in the late-1950s and early-1960s, the resident applicant pool gradually became more homogeneous regarding age and prior experience, making it easier for training chiefs to standardize the orthopedic curriculum and rotations. The increase in homogeneity resulted in large part from the institution of the Berry Plan, a "doctors draft," that influenced choices young physicians made about entering the military before or after residency training.[6]

During the 1970s and 1980s, as a result of a perceived need for more physicians, the federal government encouraged the development of new medical schools and residency training programs (including the

University of Arizona). As orthopedics became an increasingly popular surgical subspecialty, resident applications and interviews correspondingly increased. The program at the University of Arizona from 1979-85 was no exception. Selecting residents from among the exploding number of graduating medical student applicants became an extremely difficult challenge for training program chairmen and their secretarial and administrative staff members. In the early-1980s a computerized match system for medical specialty resident selection was developed, modeled after the efficient existing internship matching plan that had been in place for several years. The match system required the student to create a list of residency programs (ten or more) that he/she preferred, while the residency program faculties created a similar list of applicants they preferred. The lists were then integrated by a computer program and "matched" in compatibility.

Prior to submitting their match requests for a residency program, many applicants traveled long distances, at considerable expense, to interview for a residency position. There were often more than sixty eager applicants for two residency positions. Characteristic of his interest in an individual's honesty and personal integrity, LFP preferred to conduct an unstructured personal interview, in which any subject or topic was fair game. LFP believed that it was important for all applicants to interview with the "chief" and would often see as many as seven applicants on interview days, in addition to his clinical and administrative responsibilities. Although LFP was willing to interview all applicants scheduled, some of the other faculty were less willing to do so. LFP made a special effort to sign all rejection letters for residents not accepted into the program, as he hated rejecting applicants and believed that the least he could do was personally sign these letters.

The American Board of Orthopaedic Surgery and the Orthopaedic Residency Review Committee developed mandatory national standards for training programs, resulting in increased complexity and time requirements for program administrators. National "in-training" examinations, often described as "mock boards," were instituted in the early 1960s. They required proctoring by the administrative and clerical staff. These examinations were a method of evaluating a program and its residents against a national standard. Beginning in the 1980s, formal evaluation sessions with each resident were required after every rotation (e.g., sports medicine, pediatrics, joint replacement, spine, hand), allowing the resident to have feedback about his or her performance. A written copy of the evaluation was placed in the resident's file, accessible to the resident as well as the faculty. The Residency Review Committee members carefully scrutinized these files during their site visits, when the program was evaluated for accreditation or re-accreditation. Program evaluation occurred approximately every four years, or more frequently when there were major changes or deficiencies. Despite the demands on the time of the faculty, LFP wholeheartedly endorsed and participated in the innovative improvements and standardization of orthopedic education.

LFP summarized the extraordinary changes that occurred during his teaching career in an article entitled, "How Many Members Must an Orthopaedic Department Have to Teach Effectively?"[7] "Between 1950 and 1980, there was a spectacular growth in the breadth of orthopaedic surgery. In 1950, an orthopaedic surgeon was expected to be competent not only in the fields of adult and children's orthopaedics, but also in the field of trauma and the care of fractures. Thirty years later it was impossible for even the most ardent student to develop proficiency in all of these areas. The result was increasing specialization. These changes were reflected in the faculty at the University of Arizona Medical Center. At the time of my retirement in 1985, the faculty consisted of two surgeons doing total joint replacement, one hand surgeon, one pediatric surgeon, one sports medicine surgeon, one fracture surgeon, one back surgeon, and three general orthopedic surgeons, two of whom were at the Tucson Veterans Administration Hospital. All of these faculty members shared in teaching medical students and residents."[8]

LFP's hospital appearance was dignified, impeccable, and predictable. He wore an immaculate white laboratory coat and, throughout most of his career, a colorful bow tie. Many photographs in his early professorial years would show him mimicking Napoleon, with the fingers of his right hand thrust under the left side of his buttoned laboratory coat, and the back of his hand and his thumb visible. This continued until it was pointed out to him that Napoleon was eventually defeated. LFP nodded affirmatively at the veracity of this statement. The following day, LFP was seen to be sporting a new pair of Wellington boots. (The Duke of Wellington defeated Napoleon at Waterloo in 1815). Later on, in his Tucson years, LFP would, at times, arrive at work wearing more relaxed western attire.

LFP's communication style was straightforward and honest. "He had no time for insincere or inappropriate questions, or people who rattled on and on for effect. He had a knack for discouraging this with a very effective look, which sent people on their way in a hurry. He gave a rather formal appearance (much like an unapproachable dignitary dressed for going to the opera even when he was walking around in his scrubs) that could be impenetrable, if one didn't have the courage to approach him and find the strong, but delightful and considerate person inside."[9] His comments and words of praise were measured and sincere. Perhaps the most personally rewarding statement to hear from him consisted of three short words, "I'm so pleased"… the ultimate compliment.

LFP led by example. For instance, when things were moving more slowly than he thought necessary between cases in the operating room, instead of yelling at others, he occasionally grasped a mop and cleaned the floor himself, to demonstrate that "turnaround time" could be decreased.

LFP expected his residents to dress and behave professionally. Residents and medical students were expected to wear clean and pressed white laboratory coats, ties, have short hair, and no beards. "LFP also demanded meticulous application of plaster dressings [casts], and careful, neat wound closure. Why? Because that is all the patient sees, and if the doctor is untidy, the wound rough and irregular, and the plaster dressing poorly applied, the patient assumes his care has also been carried out in a slipshod manner."[10]

Honesty was paramount, and the importance of professional ethics was stressed. No medical student or resident tardiness for scheduled ward rounds or surgical procedures was tolerated, and no venting by residents was permitted in the operating room when things were not going well. Residents were not allowed to blame their mistakes on surgical instruments. According to LFP, "It's a poor carpenter who blames his tools." The importance of treating nurses and other support personnel as members of the professional team was emphasized. A medical student spitting tobacco juice into a wastebasket in the doctor's lounge was instantly kicked off the service. The intervention of a University of Arizona College of Medicine assistant dean failed to reinstate the student, and he finished his rotation on another surgical service. LFP elaborated, "He was kicked off the service, not for spitting in the wastebasket per se, but for thinking he could get away with it on my service." Emphasizing his commitment to professional ethics and personal integrity, when confronted with outrageous behavior, LFP would often comment, paraphrasing Winston Churchill, "There is a limit to the amount of horseshit up with which I will put."[11] If students, staff, and residents met his standard for professional demeanor, LFP was extremely loyal. If they were honest with him, LFP would support them to the hilt.

LFP emphasized good communication in both the process and the content of his teaching. He frequently employed the Socratic method[12] in the process of teaching "because it suited my personality and felt natural." A student's question was rarely answered directly with a simple fact, but instead was in turn, answered with a question. After further dialogue with LFP, the student would most often discover the correct answer and learn much more. He recognized that residents must learn to communicate concisely and accurately, both verbally and in writing. Effective communication is crucial when physicians are describing conditions and treatment plans to patients and their families, as well as in consultations with their colleagues.

LFP's intolerance of sloppy communication is demonstrated in his response to a written consultation request that simply stated "patient has an infected heal." LFP carefully made appropriate suggestions for the patient's care, but added the postscript: "Physician, *heel* thyself!"[13] He also would remind the residents that "you *apply* a plaster dressing; you *cast* a play (or dispersion)." One of his former residents from his early years commented with appreciative amusement, "LFP critiqued my construction of phrases and grammar in a paper I wrote. You see, English is not my mother tongue, but I dare say that I have practically no accent when I speak. However, when editing my papers, Dr. Peltier used to observe that, while I have no accent when I speak, I sure have one when I write!"[14]

Integral in LFP's approach to patients was his understanding of the importance of total patient care, from diagnosis through treatment and rehabilitation. He frequently reminded residents that patients often will tell you what is wrong with them if you listen carefully and ask the right questions. He would lament that focusing on the treatment of the whole patient is sometimes lost today. "Today's X-ray conferences tend to focus on the discussion of surgical procedures and types of instrumentation, with little discussion about total patient care."

Following OHW's example, LFP employed the X-ray conference as a major teaching forum. The case histories and X-rays of patients with more than one diagnosis (one obvious and others more subtle) were selected for presentation at the conference. When residents presented cases and failed to discover less obvious, but important, diagnoses, LFP, using the Socratic method, would ask pointed questions and thus facilitate the diagnostic process. Having established the diagnoses, a treatment plan was developed that incorporated a complete medical care plan, not just an orthopedic care plan.

During LFP's orthopedic career, diagnostic and surgical techniques advanced rapidly. Well aware of the continual changes, LFP incorporated "lessons" in medical history in his everyday approach to patient care, including teaching rounds, as did his mentor, OHW. He emphasized that recognizing cycles and patterns over time is valuable for the practitioner in understanding basic medical and surgical concepts. In earlier years, bones were often divided with a hand-powered osteotome (very sharp chisel) and mallet. Later, high-powered air-, electrical-, or battery-driven drills and saws were employed. Innovative diagnostic and therapeutic techniques and procedures, including computerized axial tomography (CAT scans), magnetic resonance imaging (MRIs), arthroscopy, total joint replacements, and spinal instrumentation were developed. While LFP did not emphasize particular technical operative skills, he insisted on being familiar with the surgical instruments and their application to a specific task. He stayed abreast of, and recognized the importance of, adapting to new surgical instrumentation and techniques, but he was cautious about adopting new and "unproven" procedures.

LFP was convinced that if the surgeon came to the operating room knowing what he wanted to accomplish, had selected and read about the proper procedure, understood the anatomy and was familiar with the implants and instrumentation, a good result could be anticipated. He also realized that an absolutely perfect result was not always possible, despite the best intentions. Unnecessary prolongation of operative procedures to achieve perfection, such as an anatomical result on X-ray, could increase the chance of complications. Remembering LFP's frequently used aphorism, "the enemy of good is better," a former resident commented that LFP pointed out: "life is rarely perfect, and at times the dogmatic pursuit of perfection during a difficult case can be the breeding ground for a surgical disaster."[15]

LFP was adamant that the application of brute force during an orthopedic surgical procedure was rarely successful, that finesse was more efficacious. Another former resident remembered, "I was assisting Dr. Peltier during a particularly difficult and frustrating maneuver while internally fixing a large bone fracture. While not exhibiting his frustration, he looked at me and said 'one has to be either smart, or big and strong, to be a good orthopedic surgeon and you are very big and strong!'"[16]

Throughout his career when LFP had patients in the hospital, he tried to see them in the morning before clinic, and in the evening before he left the institution. He closely and carefully observed his postoperative patients and was frequently heard to say "the price of liberty is eternal vigilance." If a potential complication appeared, it was quickly and thoroughly investigated. His approach was, "when you see a problem coming, don't duck. Run right at it!" During his patient rounds, he was accompanied by house staff and medical students, most of whom observed and adopted his philosophies.

Exemplifying the paradigm of an academic physician, who is expected to teach, have a clinical practice, and further the knowledge of the profession with investigative work, LFP had a productive research career. Early on he was very active in the laboratory, seeking to solve physiological problems through "bench" studies. Although he did not absolutely insist, he "encouraged" the residents, by his example, to take clinical problems to the laboratory. If they did not have a project of their own, they assisted in research being conducted by members of the faculty. LFP also demanded that the investigative studies be conducted carefully, according to scientific methodology. His philosophy was that one should set up the study with good controls, follow the procedures carefully for every trial, then trust the numbers that came out of it. If the investigative work merited publication, LFP insisted that the name of the resident doing the actual "hands on" research was listed as first author on the paper to be published. Technicians and students were also recognized for their contributions by being listed as authors. When one of the co-authors on a paper remarked that "so many of us are named that it appears silly," and asked him whose name should be dropped, he answered "mine."[17]

Although LFP was very busy meeting career demands, he recognized the importance of his own family, as well as the families of those with whom he worked. Throughout his career, LFP made a concerted attempt to go home to eat his evening meal, going back to the hospital after dinner, if necessary. LFP explained that, as an intern, he had been subjected to Sunday morning rounds by an agnostic faculty physician who, thus, prevented him from attending church with his family. He never forgot, and he deliberately avoided scheduling Sunday morning rounds.[18]

He and his wife, Marian, appreciated and contributed to the culture of the cities in which they resided, as well as taking an avid interest in their children and supporting them in their activities. In Minnesota their "spare" time was consumed with young children. In Kansas City, they enjoyed a variety of cultural opportunities, including regular attendance at the symphony and exploring the wide variety of available cuisines, as well as keeping up with the activities of two growing boys.

Educational pursuits were important to both Leonard and Marian. Marian studied at KU to update her knowledge base and maintain licensure in dietetics during the Kansas City years, eldest son George became a plastic surgeon, and younger son Steve became a certified public accountant (CPA). In Tucson, and in Albuquerque where they

Marian Peltier was born in Omaha, Nebraska, the daughter of an Omaha surgeon. She received her elementary and secondary education in Omaha. At the University of Nebraska in Lincoln, she joined Alpha Phi sorority and lived in the sorority house until she graduated in 1943 with a Bachelor of Science degree in dietetics. She interned for a year at the University of Minnesota Hospital and then worked at the same institution until 1945. She married LFP in the fall of 1943, and accompanied him, maintaining their home, as his career led him from university to university, and then to retirement in Albuquerque. She retained her interest in foods and nutrition throughout their married years and is an excellent cook. Hers and LFP's culinary interests are remembered by all who knew them! "Leonard and Marian always knew the best places to go out to eat!" and "Dinner at their home was always a wonderful event!"

Marian Peltier

∞

Photo courtesy of the Peltier family

resided in their later retirement years, Leonard and Marian continued their active involvement in the cities' cultural and civic activities, along with their more academic endeavors. From 1977 to 1979 LFP was a member of the Board of Directors of the Tucson Symphony Society. He also served on the City of Tucson's Health Planning Council (1974-5) and the Public Transportation Technical Citizen's Advisory Committee (1977-90).

LFP's acts of kindness extended beyond the family. Residents getting married or becoming parents all received gifts from Dr. and Mrs. Peltier. In Arizona, at Christmas, LFP personally delivered turkeys, via a borrowed gurney from the emergency room, to residents and others at the Arizona Health Sciences Center. In Kansas City, LFP and his

George Peltier was born in Minneapolis where he currently is a plastic surgeon. His elementary education was in Minnesota while his father was a resident in general and orthopedic surgery, and his secondary education was in the Kansas City area at Shawnee Mission East High School. He earned a B.A. degree in Chemistry from Lawrence University, Appleton, Wisconsin, in 1967 and an M.D. from the University of Kansas School of Medicine in 1971. He served in the United States Army Medical Corps for two years before completing his general surgery and plastic surgery residencies at the University of Kansas. He is married to Claudia, a registered nurse and a daughter of Claude Hitchcock, M.D. George has three children and two grandchildren. He is in practice at the Hennepin County Medical Center in Minneapolis, Minnesota.

George Peltier

Photo courtesy of the Peltier family

associate, Lynn Litton, M.D., initiated this tradition, engaging the popular and highly regarded Fred Wolferman's grocery to deliver a ham and a turkey to the home of each resident.

Many acquaintances of LFP have poignant memories to relate about personally experiencing his kindness and generosity. The authors of this book are no exception. In the mid-1960s FWR, then a senior resident with major responsibilities in the Kansas University residency program, received a call at mid-day that his father had had a cerebral vascular accident (stroke). FWR informed LFP that he needed to return home to Wyoming to see his dad, assess the situation and possibly assume, temporarily, his father's busy general medical practice. LFP responded, "By all means, you need to go," and immediately offered to

Stephen Peltier
∞

Steve Peltier was born in Minneapolis. He is a Certified Public Accountant in a firm that he founded in 1987 in Albuquerque, New Mexico, Peltier, Gustafson & Miller, P.A. His elementary and secondary education were in the Kansas City area in the Shawnee Mission school system. He earned a B.S. degree in accounting from the University of Kansas in 1972 and a master's degree (M.S.) in accounting from Arizona State University in 1973. He is married to Melanie (Lanie), who also was educated in the Shawnee Mission, Kansas, schools and at KU. They have three children and one grandchild.

Photo courtesy of the Peltier family

drive him to his Kansas City residence, as FWR did not have a car at work. In conversation during the trip to his home, FWR mentioned that his father had recently been honored by the Wyoming State Medical Society for civic service to his local community.[19] LFP remarked, "Doctors can certainly do a lot for a small community." As they parted, LFP said, "We want you back as soon as you can get here, we need you. But take all the time you need, because you've got to do it right!"

Janolyn Lo Vecchio similarly remembers the kindness and compassion of the Peltiers when her mother died. "I can still remember calling him from the ER to tell him of her death, and his supportive words, 'what can I do to help?' At the time of her death, I was working full-time as the administrative assistant for orthopedics, as well as attending college part-time. I had two finals scheduled a week after her funeral, which was in December. Dr. Peltier quickly approved my request for a month away from work. Dr. and Mrs. Peltier sent a large floral arrangement to my mother's funeral, and they attended the visitation and the service. A few days later a Christmas letter arrived at my house from Dr. Peltier, telling me how much I was missed at the office."

Another example of the Peltiers' empathetic understanding was demonstrated in a letter and gift to JBR. In the spring of 1992 FWR (her husband) underwent an emergency four-vessel coronary bypass that was complicated by a post-operative substernal infection. His three-month convalescence required numerous nursing treatment procedures, carried out by JBR, in the hospital and at home. In conversation with LFP several weeks later, FWR remarked "I don't think I would have pulled through if it hadn't been for JoAnn's care." LFP nodded silently, and the conversation moved to other topics. In the mail soon after, a treasured first edition of Florence Nightingale's *Notes on Nursing*, that had been owned by LFP's grandmother, arrived with the following letter:

7 December 1992

Dear JoAnn:

While I am not able to present you with a medal for what you did to help Fred during his recent illness, I am able to present you with this copy of the first American edition of Florence Nightingale, "Notes on Nursing," New York: D. Appleton and Company, 1860. It was a part of my grandmother's library which she inherited from the father of her husband, Thomas W. Chittenden, whose name can be faintly seen on the fly leaf. Please accept it in lieu of a medal and treasure it, as I have, through the years.

We enjoyed our recent visit to Kansas City and, as might be expected, continued to be surprised and impressed with all of the changes that have occurred since we left for Tucson in 1971. I am especially pleased to see what Fred has done to nurture the growth of the orthopedic section into one of the best in the country.

Marian and I join in wishing you all a very happy holiday season,

Sincerely,
Leonard F. Peltier

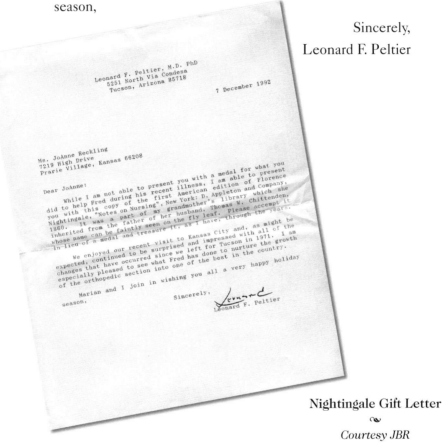

Nightingale Gift Letter
∞
Courtesy JBR

In honor of LFP's twenty-fifth anniversary as an orthopedic training chief, Ms. Lo Vecchio, with help from faculty, staff, and current and former residents at Arizona, organized a special, surprise tribute to "the professor" in Tucson. All thirty-two individuals who had completed a residency with LFP by 1982, plus the ten who were currently in his Arizona program, were invited. A total of thirty-five attended, sixteen

Celebrating LFP's 25th year as Professor and Program Chairman

Ↄ

FRONT ROW: (L to R) Robert Karpman (UA '81), Bernard Albina (KU '71), Federico
    Adler (KU '60, KU faculty), W. Robert Orr (KU '59), LFP, Wallace Holderman
    (KU '59), Thomas Peters (UA '79)
SECOND ROW: John Wertzberger (KU '68), Howard Ellfeldt (KU '68), James Dinsmore
    (KU '61), Richard Laubengayer (UA '74), Joseph Nichols (UA '78), Ernest
    Gradillas (UA '78), Melvin Roberts (KU '70)
THIRD ROW: Robert Volz (KU '64, UA Faculty), John Pazell (KU '71), Samuel Kaplan
    (KU '72), David Mayer (UA '76), Steven Cunningham (UA '75), Donald Speer
    (UA '73, UA Faculty), James Laidlaw (KU '69), Phillip Baker (KU '70)

FOURTH ROW: Michael Pitt (UA Faculty), William Quinlan (UA '83), John Medlen (UA '83), Fred Reckling (KU '64, KU faculty), Donald Spencer (KU '65), Lawrence Strathman (KU '66)

TOP ROW: George Peltier (LFP's son), Dwite Dahms (UA '84), James Benjamin (UA '84), Eric Fishman (UA '83), Robert Dzioba (UA Faculty), Leonard Mulbry (UA '85), Gerald Telep (UA '85), J. Keith Braun (UA '86), E. C. Percy (UA Faculty), Ralph Heap (UA '83)

ATTENDED REUNION BUT MISSING FROM PHOTO: William Fulcher (UA '78), Michael Parseghian (UA '86)

Photo by Biomedical Communications Department of the College of Medicine, University of Arizona, Courtesy of Janolyn Lo Vecchio of the twenty-one graduates of the Kansas program, and nineteen of the twenty-one Arizona residents or former residents. Many of their wives accompanied them. LFP's two sons, who by that time had busy careers in other states, also attended the event, surprising their unsuspecting father.

The single day event on Saturday, 24 April 1982, included a scientific program in the morning, a tour of the University of Arizona Health Sciences Center facilities in the afternoon, and a gala dinner, complete with "toasts and roasts," in the evening. LFP first realized that something unusual was taking place when he entered the auditorium that Saturday morning, expecting to deliver a lecture at anesthesiology grand rounds, and instead was greeted by a standing ovation from a room full of people! (Dr. Robert Volz had persuaded Dr. Burnell Brown, Head of the Department of Anesthesiology, to issue a bogus invitation for LFP to lecture to their group).

Surprise!

∞

Photo by Biomedical Communications Department of the College of Medicine, University of Arizona, Courtesy of Janolyn Lo Vecchio

Dr. Speer organized and moderated the scientific program, asking LFP to discuss each of the twelve scientific papers presented, including one by LFP's son George. Dr. Volz organized the dinner's agenda and invited a number of the former residents from the Kansas and Arizona programs to roast the chief. He also read congratulatory letters written by former colleagues of LFP from across the nation. And Laurel Speer delivered a touching tribute on behalf of the wives, in appreciation of LFP's attention and concern for residents' and staff members' families.

Always the Professor!

∾

LFP, FWR and Bob Volz

*Photo by Biomedical Communications Department of the College of Medicine,
University of Arizona, Courtesy of Janolyn Lo Vecchio*

The reunion provided a delightful occasion for old friends to visit with the Peltiers and each other. Because of the excellent planning and long advance notice of the event, people from several states were able to attend. One former resident showed up exactly one year early! He endured a considerable amount of ribbing from his friends, to which he replied, "Well, I was really eager to roast the chief!"[20]

Like father, like son!

❧

LFP with son George, listening to one of the speakers.

Photo by Biomedical Communications Department of the College of Medicine, University of Arizona, Courtesy of Janolyn Lo Vecchio

The success of LFP's teaching methods can be judged by their outcome. He related that, "of forty-eight residents I trained, only one did not obtain board certification. The majority went into private general orthopedic practice or one of the orthopedic subspecialties and served their communities in Kansas, Arizona, and elsewhere. Seven residents entered academic practice (Drs. Adler, Benjamin, Quinlan, Reckling, Speer, Valencia and Volz), and three became program chairmen (Benjamin, Reckling and Volz). Four became members of the prestigious American Orthopaedic Association (Karpman, Reckling, Speer, and Volz)."

The Party's Over

Jim Benjamin, Marian and LFP

Photo by Biomedical Communications Department of the College of Medicine, University of Arizona, Courtesy of James Benjamin and Janolyn Lo Vecchio, Modified by Carol Stevens

Notes and Sources

1. Leonard F. Peltier, M.D., Ph.D., and J. Bradley Aust, M.D., Ph.D., *L'Étoile du Nord, An Account of Owen Harding Wangensteen (1898-1981)*, (Chicago: American College of Surgeons, 1994), p. 76.

2. Philip H. Krutzsch, Ph.D., Professor Emeritus, Department of Cell Biology and Anatomy, University of Arizona Health Sciences Center, letter to JGL, November 28, 1999.

3. Federico Adler, M.D. (KU '60), personal communication to FWR, December 2003.

4. Essay by Laurel Speer, 1997.

5. W. Robert Orr, M.D. (KU '59), letter to JGL, Fall 1999.

6. Frank B. Berry, "The story of 'The Berry Plan,'" *Bulletin of the New York Academy of Medicine* 52 (1976): 278-82. In the aftermath of the Korean War, there were not enough interns and residents to satisfy the needs of both military and civilian hospitals. If the military had been allowed to draft all the young physicians it needed, the pool of resident applicants for training programs would have been extremely small, and the military would have had a cadre of young, minimally-trained physicians, but not an adequate number of specialists. To stabilize this situation and provide a fair solution for all, Frank B. Berry, M.D., who held the office at that time entitled "Assistant Secretary of Defense for Health," created the Berry Plan. This plan permitted young physicians to choose among three options: (1) entering the armed services immediately after internship and returning to their residencies after service; (2) entering the armed services two years after medical school and completing their residencies after service; and (3) entering the service after the completion of residency training. Most selected options one or three. Although young physicians had the option of not registering for the Berry Plan, they would then be subject to their own local Selective Service Boards. Conventional wisdom was that the Berry Plan was a wiser choice. During the Plan's twenty-plus years of existence, 23,000 young physicians served their country in the military.

7. Leonard F. Peltier, "How Many Members Must an Orthopaedic Department Have to Teach Effectively?" *Clinical Orthopaedics and Related Research* 385 (2001):13-5.

8. Ibid., p. 14.

9. Marian Kuenzig, letter to JGL, October 29, 1999. Marian was LFP's lab technician at the University of Kansas from approximately 1960 to 1971.

10. Howard Ellfeldt, M.D. (KU '68), letter to JGL, Fall 1999.

11. James C. Humes, *The Wit & Wisdom of Winston Churchill*, (New York: Harper-Perennial, 1995), p. 198. "A priggish civil servant had corrected and returned a Churchill memorandum, pointing out that the prime minister had mistakenly ended a sentence with a preposition. Back it went to the officious bureaucrat, with this Churchill note appended in the margin. 'This is the sort of pedantic nonsense up with which I will not put.'"

12. The crux of the Socratic method is that the teacher should, by patient questioning, bring the pupil to recognize some true conclusion, without the teacher's telling the pupil that that conclusion is true. A. Flew, *A Dictionary of Philosophy*, second edition (New York: St. Martin's Press, 1979), p. 330.

13. Frederick W. Reckling, M.D. (KU '64), letter to JGL, Fall 1999.

14. Federico Adler, M.D. (KU '60), letter to JGL, Fall 1999.

15. James B. Benjamin, M.D. (UA '84), letter to JGL, Fall 1999.

16. John Wertzberger, M.D. (KU '68), letter to JGL, Fall 1999.

17. Kuenzig letter, Fall 1999.

18. LFP, personal communication to JGL.

19. "A. S. Robins Drug Company award for community service." *Lusk Herald*, Lusk, WY, September 6, 1962, p. 1.

20. James Laidlaw, M.D. (KU '69), verbal "roast" at 25th celebration, April 22, 1982, transcribed from audiotape supplied by JGL.

Teaching Publications

Leonard F. Peltier, Robert H. Geertsma and Roger L. Youmans, "Editorial: Television Videotape Recordings for Teaching Emergency Medical Care," *Journal of Trauma* 9 (1969): 823.

Leonard F. Peltier, Robert H. Geertsma and Roger L. Youmans, "Television Videotape Recording: An Adjunct in Teaching Emergency Medical Care," *Surgery* 66 (1969): 233-6.

Frederick W. Reckling, Arlo S. Hermreck and Leonard F. Peltier, "The Trauma Conference: A Method of Teaching Management of the Injured Patient," *Journal of Trauma* 14 (1974): 841-7.

Leonard F. Peltier, "A Capite ad Calcem: A Parable for Our Time," *Journal of Trauma* 21 (1981): 96-8. (Presidential Address, American Association for the Surgery of Trauma 1980).

Leonard F. Peltier, "How Many Members Must an Orthopaedic Department Have to Teach Effectively?" *Clinical Orthopaedics and Related Research* 385 (2001): 13-5.

CHAPTER SIX

Trauma

"Have we reached a point when the attractions and rewards of specialty practice are causing us to neglect one of our primary and basic obligations, the care of injured patients?"[1]

— LEONARD F. PELTIER, M.D., PH.D.

*L*FP's enthusiasm for the care of the injured patient began when he became chief of surgery of a 500-bed military hospital in post-World War II Germany. The majority of patients had sustained traumatic injuries, primarily fractures and associated soft-tissue damage, and the challenges they presented were to have a lasting impact on LFP's career. When he returned to the general surgery residency program at the University of Minnesota, he continued to encounter patients with fractures and welcomed an opportunity to obtain further training in orthopedic surgery. Although general surgeons had traditionally managed fractures, they were beginning to limit their trauma focus to the repair of damaged blood vessels and other soft tissue injuries of the extremities and abdominal and thoracic cavities. Orthopedic surgeons began to assume major responsibility for fracture management.

LFP's postgraduate training in both disciplines (general and orthopedic surgery) provided him with a broad spectrum of expertise in trauma care. During his residency and early faculty years in Minnesota, in addition to patient care, research, and teaching, he published four trauma-related articles in professional journals. While in Kansas and Arizona he continued his interest in injured patients and was instrumental in improving and standardizing their care. In Kansas he established a weekly multidisciplinary trauma conference and videotaped real-life trauma situations in the emergency room for purposes of teaching and evaluating trauma care (see Kansas chapter for details).

When LFP moved to Arizona in 1971, he had the opportunity to organize the trauma care program at the new University of Arizona (UA) Medical Center and influence the management of injured patients in the city of Tucson and surrounding counties in southern Arizona. As he had done in Kansas, he established a UA weekly trauma conference, treated many trauma patients, worked with other physicians in the city to improve trauma care for the community, and continued publishing trauma-related articles in the medical literature. At UA medical center he was a member of the Disaster Committee (1971-5) and the Trauma Committee (1985-90). He also served on the city of Tucson's Emergency Services Council (1973-5) and the Pima County Blue Ribbon Advisory Committee on Emergency Health Care (1978-90).

LFP became recognized nationally, as well as locally, for his expertise in the management of injured patients, not only as an orthopedic surgeon, but also from a general societal perspective. From 1972 to 1981 he served on the American College of Surgeons (ACS)[2] Committee on Trauma, a national multidisciplinary committee of the ACS that included general, vascular, orthopedic, and neurosurgeons. As a member of this committee, LFP played an integral role in the development of national guidelines designed to optimize the care of trauma patients in the United States. Trauma care was changing rapidly with the advent of the 911 telephone emergency notification system, better-trained emergency medical technicians, helicopter evacuation, and the creation of trauma centers as we know them today. Professional surgical organization members recognized that a system to evaluate and standardize the management of the injured patient was sorely needed. Assuming this responsibility, the ACS Committee on Trauma planned and initiated a process, a form of which is still in place today, whereby trauma centers can receive national designation for the care they provide, based on the severity of the patient's injuries and the resources of the facility to treat those injuries.

Designation as a trauma center is voluntary, rather than mandated, but is sought by many hospitals. To achieve this designation, an institution requests consultation and verification of its potential for meeting performance criteria for one of four levels of trauma care.[3] Level I trauma centers (the highest level) have the capacity for providing total care for every aspect of injury, from prevention through rehabilitation. Additionally, they must include a trauma registry and research program, and thus are usually located in teaching hospitals where research support is available. Level II trauma centers have the capacity for providing total care for every aspect of injury, but do not include a research program. Trauma centers with Levels III and IV designations are able to provide less complex care, but can offer immediate resuscitative care, with transfer to a higher-level center when needed. Local emergency responders are trained to assess injured patients and determine the level of care needed, as well as to provide transport to the optimum trauma center for each situation.

Drawing on his national experience in standardizing care for trauma patients, LFP remained active in securing optimum care for the citizens of southern Arizona. After the tragic Pioneer Hotel fire in Tucson on 20 December 1970,[4] the Tucson Disaster Committee was formed to develop a city-wide disaster plan. Simulated disasters were staged to provide on-scene training for emergency personnel. Plans and procedures were developed to coordinate transport of injured patients to appropriate facilities for further resuscitation and follow-up care. The facilities developed plans to quickly summon and assemble emergency resources (equipment and personnel) that might be needed in unusual circumstances. However, in spite of these "front-line" efforts, Tucson did not have a designated trauma center by the early 1980s.

LFP recognized the need for a Level I trauma center in Tucson and worked with the local medical community to achieve this designation for the Arizona Health Sciences Center (AHSC). As is often the case in developing a facility that will attract patients to an institution, political negotiation was part of the three-year process to bring the trauma center to reality.

LFP elaborated: "In Tucson several doctors were interested in developing a trauma center…when Level I national standards were created, the process became easier. [Among other requirements] Level I standards required a hospital to have a full-time general surgeon for the emergency room and a neurosurgeon [available on an 'on call' status]. All the Tucson hospitals initially wanted to become Level I trauma centers, but eventually they all pulled out except for the University Medical Center and Tucson Medical Center [TMC]. Esther Capin, a member of the Board of Directors of the Arizona Health Sciences Center, hired a facilitator to coordinate the planning process. Although I thought the facilitator was unnecessary at first, in time he proved very helpful.

"Kino Hospital would have been the ideal place for the trauma center for the whole city and [it] had lots of empty beds. But there was no money for upgrading the facilities. The county wouldn't spend the money, so instead of a single center, a very peculiar arrangement evolved. The two hospitals, Tucson Medical Center and the Arizona Health Sciences Center, were designated as a Level I Trauma Center with two [participating institutions]. The initial agreement was that the two hospitals would pool all patient care results [to meet the research requirements of a Level I center], and it would be a cooperative agreement.

"Then the chief operating officer of Tucson Medical Center made an exclusive deal with the Department of Public Safety for helicopter service to bring patients only to Tucson Medical Center. He also hired a trauma director to run his center without consulting the University. The original plan for cooperation began to deteriorate." Fortunately, the situation was eventually reconciled, and TMC and the AHSC cooperated to run a Level I trauma center based at two facilities.

Long after LFP's retirement, the care of injured patients remains a national and local health concern, and on 1 July 2003 Tucson Medical Center stopped offering Level I trauma care due to high operating costs, leaving AHSC as southern Arizona's only Level I trauma center.[5] Under this arrangement, when AHSC is nearing capacity, community hospitals agree to take the less-seriously-injured trauma patients.

In addition to LFP's national responsibilities with the ACS Committee on Trauma, he accepted a position on the Board of Managers of the American Association for the Surgery of Trauma (AAST)[6] in 1975 and remained on that board until 1983. He served as national president of the AAST in 1980-1. In 1997 LFP reminisced about his presidential year: "As president of the AAST, my chief accomplishment was broadening and opening up the membership. The AAST began in the 1930s, and there had been the same number of members for years…250-300 at the time of my presidency." Although the only formally stated requirement for membership in the AAST was membership in the American College of Surgeons, when LFP assumed the presidency it was, in reality, a highly selective, inbred group of people, primarily general surgeons, and its numbers were far smaller than the many thousands in the American Academy of Orthopaedic Surgeons[7] and the American College of Surgeons.[8] The AAST general surgeons were being challenged in their domain of caring for trauma patients by orthopedic surgeons, anesthesiologists who managed pulmonary complications of chest trauma, and physicians in the newer specialties of emergency medicine, trauma surgery, and critical care medicine. LFP was successful in convincing the association to increase its numbers as well as to welcome physicians in all the specialties and subspecialties interested in care of the multiply-injured patient.

He also initiated changes in the membership terms of the AAST Board of Managers. Originally, a board member served two two-year terms followed by one nine-year term as an observer. LFP was able to limit the length of time that board members served to three two-year terms, thus allowing for more turnover and diversity in ideas within the organization's management team.

"The year of my presidency was an interesting time in my life because I was 60 years old. I was unsure whether or not to buy a new tuxedo because I didn't know if I would ever wear it again. The new tuxedo that I bought as president has subsequently been worn regularly."

LFP planned the fortieth annual meeting of the American Association for the Surgery of Trauma, 18-20 September 1980, his presidential year, at the Biltmore Hotel in Phoenix, Arizona. He invited Carl T. Brighton, M.D., a prominent orthopedic surgeon who was an expert in the electrical stimulation of fracture healing, to present the keynote address.[9] In keeping with LFP's interest in history, he selected an historical painting, "Operation Arrowhead," by a local artist, Ettore "Ted" De Grazia, for the meeting's program cover.

Operation Arrowhead

∽

Ettore "Ted" De Grazia

Image used with permission of the De Grazia Foundation© 2004

"Operation Arrowhead," part of the Cabeza de Vaca collection painted by De Grazia in 1973 and housed at the Gallery in the Sun in Tucson,[10] depicts the first surgery (removal of an arrowhead) carried out by a European on the North American continent. Alvar Nuñez Cabeza de Vaca, a native of Portugal, was one of the first Europeans to explore the North American Continent. Nuñez came from landed gentry with a long military tradition. The surname, Cabeza de Vaca (head of a cow), originated as a title of honor following the Battle of Las Navas de Tolorosa on 12 July 1212, during the wars between the Christians and Moors, when a peasant marked an unguarded mountain pass with a cow's skull.[11]

Nuñez and three associates were the only survivors of a group cast ashore on Galveston Island off the south Texas coast in November 1527. They progressed through West Texas, across New Mexico, and into Southeastern Arizona over a ten-year period from 1527-36, and became known as "healers." Nuñez became the surgeon of the group, and somewhere in New Mexico he performed what he refers to as: "My Famous Operation in the Mountain Country."[12]

In his presidential address, entitled "A Capite ad Calcem: [From Head to Foot] A Parable for Our Time,"[13] reprinted here as well as in the *Journal of Trauma*,[14] LFP retold the story of this first operation carried out by a European in the southwestern United States.

In his typical scholarly and perceptive way, LFP related ancient history in the surgery of trauma to contemporary problems, noting that "surgeons continue to deal with problems presented by injured patients…Whether it be 500 years in our own region, or 5,000 years in the history of the world, these problems have remained surprisingly constant." Aware of the attractions and rewards of a narrowly-focused specialty practice, he reiterated his belief that physicians must not lose their understanding of the importance of the wider scope of care of the injured patient, and that they must be eternally vigilant about the possibility of "a fiat by an outside agency [the church, in medieval times] without a real stake or role in the practice of medicine" profoundly affecting patient care.

LFP's position on the Board of Managers of the AAST led to his appointment to represent the AAST on the much larger American College of Surgeons Board of Governors from 1980 to1986. He served as Vice-Chairman of the board during the last three years of his term.

The ACS has a two-tiered management structure: it is governed by a nineteen-member Board of Regents, and the Regents are elected by the 275-member Board of Governors. To provide balanced geographical representation, two-thirds of the Governors are nominated by the membership-at-large and elected during an annual meeting of Fellows during the Clinical Congress. Certain surgical societies, chapters, and federal medical services are permitted to nominate Governors up to a level of one-third of the members of the Board of Governors.[15]

LFP described his experience: "The Board of Governors of the American College of Surgeons is like the House of Lords [in the English Parliament] because all the power resides in the ACS Board of Regents. Some members are elected and others represent specific societies. I became a member because I represented the AAST." In reality, while the Board of Governors does not have direct power, it is an active group of physicians who work together on a variety of committees and make recommendations to the Board of Regents for issues that need to be addressed.

In addition to all of his other activities during his career at Arizona, LFP was a member from 1972 to 1982 of the ACS Committee on Postgraduate Education, another national committee that has had a lasting impact on the quality of medical education and patient care. On this committee he participated in creating the first home study program designed to help surgeons maintain a sound and current knowledge base in clinical surgery. The Surgical Education and Self-Assessment Program, commonly referred to as SESAP, provides practicing surgeons an opportunity to stay abreast of current standards in surgical practice by completing the home study program. The program (paper manual or CD-rom) simulates, in written form, the diagnostic and treatment challenges faced in the practice of surgery, enabling the surgeon to make choices and follow decision-trees to programmed outcomes. Appropriate choices result in good outcomes, poor choices in poor outcomes. The SESAP is used also as a study guide by candidates for the American Board of Surgery certification and recertification exams, and as a Continuing Medical Education (CME) product for surgeons throughout the world.[16] "I helped to develop the [first] SESAP surgical education

American College of Surgeons Board of Governors Officers
October 1984

∾

(L to R) Leonard F. Peltier, Tucson, AZ, Vice-Chairman
Joe Bradley Aust, San Antonio, TX, Chairman
James L. Talbert, Gainesville, FL, Secretary

Photo courtesy of J. Bradley Aust

test for surgeons preparing for the board examinations. No one had ever done it before and it was a fascinating experience. We had to write questions and give references. We discovered that the best way was to find a good reference and then write the question."

LFP's interest in care for injured patients included laboratory investigation. Early in his career he took a trauma-related clinical problem, fat embolism, to the research bench, in the tradition established by his mentor, OHW. His pioneering investigative findings, alongside his comprehensive approach to hands-on trauma care provided a foundation for improved management of the multiply-injured patient.

A Capite ad Calcem- A Parable for Our Time (1980 A.A.S.T Presidential Address)*

∾

Leonard F. Peltier, M.D., Ph.D.

A life filled with hazard compelled the indigenous populations of the American Southwest to develop methods of treating injuries. The same skilled hands that fashioned tools, baskets, pottery, and textiles, fashioned splints of wood and yucca, padded with down, moss, or fur, and bound them into place with strips of hide or woven cotton. The sophistication of their surgical procedures can be appreciated from the evidence of successful trephination.

The first Europeans entered the Sonoran Desert between 1528 and 1536. They were four survivors of the expedition of Panfilo Narvaez who sailed from Cuba with 600 men in 1527 to explore Florida and the northern coast of the Gulf of Mexico. One of these men, Alvar Nuñez Cabeza de Vaca, performed the first operation carried out by a European in this region. The description of this case, translated from his own narrative deserves to be repeated.

> "Here they brought to me a man who, they told, a long time ago had been shot through the left side of the back with an arrow the head of which stuck close to his heart. He said it gave him much pain, and that on this account, he was sick. I touched the region of the body and felt the arrowhead, and that it had pierced the cartilage. So with a knife I cut open the breast as far as the place. The arrow point had gotten athwart, and was very difficult to remove. By cutting deeper and inserting the point of the knife with great difficulty I got it out; it was very long. Then with a deer bone, according to my knowledge of surgery, I made two stitches. After

---

*Reprinted with permission of Lippincott, Williams & Wilkins © from the *Journal of Trauma* 21, 2 (1981)

I had extracted the arrow they begged me for it, and I gave it to them. The whole village came back to look at it and they sent it further inland that the people there might see it also.

"On account of this cure they made many dances and festivities, as is their custom. The next day I cut the stitches, and the Indian was well. The cut I had made only showed a scar like a line in the palm of the hand and he said that he felt not the least pain" (1).

During the ensuing 350 years, the mixture of adventurers, soldiers, settlers, and Indians provided a continuing experience for trauma surgeons. The most notable of these was Doctor George Goodfellow who practiced in Tombstone in the 1880's and who has been hailed by Donald D. Trunkey as "the first civilian trauma surgeon" (13). With the passage of another 100 years, we find little change. Arizona surgeons continue to deal with problems presented by injured patients. Indeed, whether it be 500 years in our own region or 5,000 years in the history of the world, these problems have remained surprisingly constant.

This is in marked contrast to the problems faced by physicians. Within the last few years we have seen disappearance of smallpox and the emergence of Legionnaire's disease. In our generation we have seen the control of poliomyelitis and tuberculosis. Rheumatoid arthritis, an important disease in our time, was unknown until the industrial revolution. There has been and continues to be a constant variation in disease processes (6). On the other hand, the constancy, indeed immutability, of patterns of injury is readily apparent to any student of the history of surgery.

The patients described by Imhotep in the Edwin Smith papyrus (11), are similar to those seen in our Emergency Departments. This document, the oldest known surgical manuscript, dates from almost 3,000 B.C. It describes accurately a series of patients with injuries, beginning with those of the head and progressing distally. The technique described for the reduction of a dislocation of the mandible is still preferred today. The order of presentation, from the head to the foot, has characterized the organization of fracture texts ever since. The title of this parable, *a capite ad calcem*, emphasizes the constancy of this tradition.

Hippocrates (460-370 B.C.) stands in relation to our time, in the same way he stood to Imhotep. His descriptions of injuries such as dislocations of the shoulder also correspond to our experience. It is doubtful if the injuries treated by Galen A.D. 131-201 in Pergamon 500 years later would seem unfamiliar to us. This unchanging nature of the patterns of injury can be appreciated easily by looking at a series of illustrations of a technique for reducing an anterior dislocation of the shoulder first described by Hippocrates (8). The first of these is one of the earliest illustrations of a surgical procedure and dates from the eighth century. The illustrations were repeated in medieval manuscripts and appeared in print for the first time in 1544. It was used by a variety of authors including Paré, Scultetus, Heister, Bell, and Astley Cooper, all of whom were treating the same injury by essentially the same method. The words and music remained the same, only the instruments and orchestration changed; and occasionally the orchestra conductor.

The medieval church became the repository of knowledge following the fall of the Roman Empire of the West. It preserved what little learning there was in Europe during a very tumultuous and difficult period. Because of this clerical orders became the only routes to literacy and education available to ambitious individuals. It is not surprising that clerics at all levels of the church hierarchy engaged in the practice of medicine. Women were not excluded from this work, and some like Hildegaard of Bingen (1098-1179) were well known (10). The medieval church had an important role in the founding of hospitals. L'Hôtel Dieu was founded in Paris in the seventh century by St. Landry, Bishop of Paris; St. Bartholomew's Hospital in London in 1123 by Rahere, the first Prior of the Priory of Austin Canons in Smithfield, to name but two. Nursing orders of women were a natural and persisting development. The Crusades saw the growth of orders such as the Knights Hospitalers who were dedicated to the care of the sick and wounded.

The very success of these churchly physicians was their undoing. They became more interested in their practice than their preaching. They were caught up in the worldly aspects of material gain, fine clothes, servants, wine, food, and the temptations of the flesh. They lost interest in the spiritual, their vows of poverty, and in the mortification of the flesh. They became preoccupied with the things of this world, rather than of the next. The result of these abuses was drastic reform.

The reform of medical practice was only a small part of a larger program which affected all of the practices and addressed all of the abuses of the clergy. It was instituted by a series of church councils held between 1130 and 1247. [The Councils of Clermont (1130), Rheims (1131), the Second Lateran (1139), Montpellier (1162), Tours (1163), Paris (1212), the Fourth Lateran (1215), and Le Mans (1247).] The reforms were expressed as canons, from the Greek word meaning a rod, a line, or a ruler. This term carried a secondary meaning of straightness, fixity, norm, or standard. The term was used by early Christian theologians to define the church's position in matters of faith and practice, dogma and discipline. Canons were designed to straighten out, literally, deviations from correct behavior and to keep wayward and rebellious clerics and parishioners in line (2-4, 7, 9, 12). Some of these canons forbade clerics to practice or even to study medicine. The practice of surgery, in particular, was proscribed. The dictum, *ecclesia abhorret a sanguine*, was observed throughout Europe, with a few notable exceptions. Among these were some of the most important surgeons of the period; Hugh of Lucca, Bruno, Theodoric, Arnold of Villanova, William of Salicet, Lanfranc, Henri de Mondeville, and Guy de Chauliac (14). Two physicians even became pope; John XXI (1276-1277) and Paul II (1464-1471) (5). In spite of these exceptions surgery as part of the intellectual mainstream of the medical life and thought ceased to exist. Rushing to fill the gap left by the departure of the educated surgeon came the self-taught specialists and quacks, the bone setters, the lithotomists, the oculists, and herniotomists. As a result of these church reforms, precipitated by the abuses of its practitioners, surgery and surgeons were forced into a decline which lasted almost 500 years. A fiat by an outside agency without a real stake or role in the practice of medicine had profoundly affected patient care.

Although Paré, a surgeon of the short robe, began the work of bringing surgery up to a level, socially and intellectually, on a par with medicine, it was not until the end of the eighteenth century that surgeons such as Pott, the Hunters, and Desault began to achieve such equality for their specialty. The practice of surgery during the nineteenth century, which saw the introduction of anesthesia, antisepsis and asepsis, and the X-ray, remained the surgery of trauma and of other urgent life-threatening conditions. The surgery of trauma remained a major central area of surgical practice until after World War II. Since then it has been eclipsed by the marvelous technical and physiologic advances which have encouraged the diversification of surgery into highly specialized enclaves far removed from trauma. As a result, the treatment of the injured patient is no longer a core subject in many surgical training programs.

Many surgeons have found that a practice consisting of the repetition of an elective, highly specialized technical procedure is so much easier and more rewarding that they have removed their names from Emergency Department call rosters. Many hospital administrators de-emphasize trauma at their hospitals because it disrupts an orderly elective surgical schedule and because the care of seriously injured patients is expensive. In the face of increasing costs of practice, including high malpractice insurance premiums, altruism, as a characteristic virtue of physicians, is vanishing rapidly. For example, in my own community during a planning exercise for a disaster drill, one surgeon expressed reluctance to respond to a disaster call unless some provision was made to reimburse him for time lost out of his office.

Are we reaching a point when the attractions and rewards of specialty practice are causing us to neglect one of our primary and basic obligations, the care of the injured patient? I believe that we are. If this is so, what kind of a denouement can we anticipate?

When surgeons are no longer responsive to the needs of the injured patient, we can look for action from outside of our group and even from outside of medicine itself, which will legislate, direct, or fiat that the care of the injured become the responsibility of others. Many of these "others" are already waiting in the wings; the EMT's, the paramedics, the emergency physicians. All of these less qualified groups are aggressively nibbling at the hems of our long white coats. Unless we show renewed interest, dedication and responsiveness to the needs of injured patients, we may find that we have been denied this role and as surgeons are left once more with a short robe.

REFERENCES

1. Cabeza de Vaca, A. N.: *The Journey of Alvar Nuñez Cabeza de Vaca, Translated from his own Narrative by Fanny Bandolier*. Chicago, The Rio Grande Press, 1964, pp. 140-141.

2. Castiglioni, Arturo: *A History of Medicine*. New York, Alfred A. Knopf, 1941, pp. 320-321.

3. Delaunay, Paul: *La Medicine et l'Eglise*. Paris, Editions Hippocrate, 1948.

4. Diepgen, Paul: Uber den Einfluss der autoritativen Theologie auf die Medizin des Mittelalters. *Abhandlungen der Geistes- und Sozialwissenschaftlichen Klasse*, Jahrgang 1958, Nr.1, pp. 1-20.

5. Garrison, Fielding H.: *An Introduction to the History of Medicine*. Philadelphia & London, Saunders, 1929, pp. 168-169.

6. Hudson, R. P.: How Diseases Birth and Die. *Transactions Studies of the College of Physicians of Philadelphia*, 45: 18-27, 1977.

7. Hughes, P.: *The Church in Crisis: A History of the General Councils* 325-1870. Garden City, New York, Hanover House, Doubleday, 1961.

8. Peltier, L. F.: The continuity of orthopedic thought and representation. *Clin. Orthop.*, 89: 106-111, 1972.

9. Schroeder, H. J.: *Disciplinary Decrees of the General Councils, Text, Translation and Commentary*. St. Louis and London, B. Herder Book Co., 1937.

10. Singer, Charles: *The Visions of Hildegard of Bingen: From Magic to Science, Essays on the Scientific Twilight*. New York, Dove, Publications, 1958.

11. *The Edwin Smith Papyrus* (translation and commentary by James Henry Breasted). Chicago, University of Chicago Press, 1930.

12. Somerville, R.: *Pope Alexander III and the Council of Tours, (1163).* Berkeley, Los Angeles, London, Univ. of California Press, 1977.

13. Trunkey, D. D.: Doctor George Goodfellow, the first civilian trauma surgeon. *Surg. Gynecol. Obstet.,* 141: 97-104, 1975.

14. Zimmerman, L. M., Veith, Ilza: *Great Ideas in the History of Surgery.* Baltimore, Williams & Wilkins, 1961, p. 100.

Notes and Sources

ᕽ

1. Leonard F. Peltier, "A Capite ad Calcem: A Parable for Our Time (1980 A.A.S.T. Presidential Address)," *Journal of Trauma*, 21, 2 (February, 1981): 96-8.

2. The American College of Surgeons (ACS) is a scientific and educational association of surgeons that was founded in 1913 to improve the quality of care for surgical patients by setting high standards for surgical education and practice. Members of the ACS are referred to as "Fellows." The letters FACS after a surgeon's name mean that the surgeon's education and training, professional qualifications, surgical competence, and ethical conduct have passed a rigorous evaluation, and have been found to be consistent with the high standards established and demanded by the College. In 2003 the College had more than 64,000 Fellows, including more than 3,700 Fellows in other countries, making it the largest organization of surgeons in the world. www.facs.org

3. American College of Surgeons Trauma Consultation and Verification Mission Statement, www.facs.org/trauma/ntdbacst.html

4. David J. Cieslak, "The Blaze Shocked the City, Hastened Downtown's Decline," *Tucson Citizen*, www.tucsoncitizen.com/history The Pioneer International Hotel in downtown Tucson burned on 20 December 1970, in a deliberately-set fire. Twenty-nine people died, some jumping from windows in the eleven-story building. The disaster provoked major changes in building codes, as well as emergency care, in the Tucson area.

5. Anne T. Denogean, "One-site Trauma System Doing OK," *Tucson Citizen*, July 8, 2003, www.tucsoncitizen.com

6. The American Association for the Surgery of Trauma (AAST) promotes the exchange of scientific information regarding all phases of care of the trauma patient. This includes prevention activities, prehospital care, resuscitation, operative care, critical care, rehabilitation and trauma system design. The AAST in the year 2003 had approximately 1000 members from a variety of trauma-related specialties and subspecialties. The official publication of the AAST is the *Journal of Trauma*. www.aast.org

7. The American Academy of Orthopaedic Surgeons (AAOS) provides education and practice management services for orthopedic surgeons and allied health professionals. The Academy also serves as an advocate for improved patient care and informs the public about the science of

orthopedics. Founded at Northwestern University as a not-for-profit organization in 1933, the Academy has grown from a small organization serving fewer than 500 members to the world's largest medical association of musculoskeletal specialists. In 2003 the Academy served about 24,000 members internationally. Fellows have completed four years of medical school and at least five years of an approved residency in orthopedics. In addition, they must pass comprehensive oral and written examinations, be certified by the American Board of Orthopaedic Surgery, and submit to stringent membership review processes prior to admission to the Academy. www.aaos.org

8. American College of Surgeons. www.facs.org

9. Carl T. Brighton, M.D., Ph.D., "Treatment of Nonunion of the Tibia with Constant Direct Current (1980 Fitts Lecture, A.A.S.T.)," *Journal of Trauma*, 21, 3 (March, 1981): 189-95.

10. Gallery in the Sun Permanent Exhibits, Tucson, AZ. www.degrazia.org

11. Leonard F. Peltier, M.D., "Cabeza de Vaca, The First European to Practice Medicine in North America Travels Through Arizona," *Sombrero* (October 1994): 13-5.

12. *Cabeza de Vaca's Adventures in the Unknown Interior of America*, a new translation, with annotation, by Cyclone Covey (New York: Collier Books, 1961).

13. "A Capite ad Calcem," translated "from head to foot," characterizes the way fracture texts have been organized from the time of Imhotep, approximately 3,000 B.C., (i.e., with injuries to the head at the beginning, progressing to injuries of the feet at the end). LFP's reference to the contrast between "surgeons" and "physicians" in the fourth and fifth paragraphs of the address, respectively, calls our attention to the reality of earlier times when surgeons were not nearly as highly educated as other physicians, and thus were usually not awarded the title of "physician." Another reference to this difference in education is his reference to "Paré, a surgeon of the short robe," reminding the reader that Paré was known to lack academic credentials, even though he was designated a master surgeon by Henri II, based on his merit (Albert S. Lyons and R. Joseph Petrucelli,II, *Medicine, An Illustrated History*, New York: Abradale Press, Harry N. Abrams, Inc. Publishers, 1987, p. 381).

14. Peltier, "A Capite ad Calcem: A Parable for Our Time."

15. American College of Surgeons, Board of Governors. www.facs.org/about/governors

16. American College of Surgeons SESAP No. 11 information (Note: the exam is now in its eleventh version). www.facs.org/fellows_info/sesap

Trauma Publications

❧

Leonard F. Peltier, "The Treatment of Fractures of the Shaft of the Femur by Intramedullary Nailing," *Bulletin of University of Minnesota Hospitals and Minnesota Medical Foundation* 22 (1952): 445-51.

Leonard F. Peltier, "The Treatment of Open (Compound) Fractures," *GP* 34, 7 (July 1954).

Leonard F. Peltier, "Emergency Management of Dislocations, Sprains and Strains," *Lancet* 74 (1954): 471-2.

Leonard F. Peltier, "Fractures of the Pelvis: A Report of 80 Cases Treated at the University Hospitals," *Minnesota Medicine* 38 (1955): 563-5.

Leonard F. Peltier, "Editorial: The Treatment of Fractures," *Surgery Gynecology and Obstetrics* 109 (1959): 376-7.

Andres Grisolia, W. J. Forrest, and Leonard F. Peltier, "The Treatment of Fractures Complicated by Burns: An Experimental Study," *Journal of Trauma* 3 (1963): 259-65.

Lynn O. Litton and Leonard F. Peltier, *Athletic Injuries* (Boston: Little Brown and Co., 1963).

Leonard F. Peltier, "Editorial: Athletic Injuries," *Minnesota Medicine* 45 (1963): 561-5.

Leonard F. Peltier, and Robert G. Volz, "Fractures of the Dorsolumbar Spine Uncomplicated by Injury of the Spinal Cord," *International Abstracts of Surgery* 116 (1963): 205-12.

Leonard F. Peltier, "Complications Associated with Fractures of the Pelvis," *Journal of Bone and Joint Surgery* 47-A (1965): 1060-9.

Andres Grisolia, Robert L. Bell and Leonard F. Peltier, "Fractures and Dislocations of the Spine Complicating Ankylosing Spondylitis," *Journal of Bone and Joint Surgery* 49-A (1967): 339-44.

Leonard F. Peltier, "Complications of Pelvic Fractures," *Hospital Medicine* 3 (1967): 88-93.

Leonard F. Peltier, "Some Complications of Fractures," *Current Problems in Surgery* (May 1967): 1-44.

John J. Wertzberger and Leonard F. Peltier, "Supracondylar Fractures: Experience with the Treatment of Patients with Supracondylar Fracture of the Femur," *Journal of the Kansas Medical Society* 68, 8 (1967): 328-39.

Leonard F. Peltier, Robert H. Geertsma and Roger L. Youmans, "Editorial: Television Videotape Recordings for Teaching Emergency Medical Care," *Journal of Trauma* 9 (1969): 823.

Leonard F. Peltier, Robert H. Geertsma and Roger L. Youmans, "Television Videotape Recording: An Adjunct in Teaching Emergency Medical Care," *Surgery* 66, 1 (1969): 233-6.

Frederick W. Reckling and Leonard F. Peltier, "Acute Knee Dislocations and Their Complications," *Journal of Trauma* 9, 3 (1969): 181-91.

R. H. Geertsma and Leonard F. Peltier, "Videotape Recording of Emergency Room Care," *Med. Biol. Illus.* 20, 1 (1970): 13-7.

Donald P. Speer and Leonard F. Peltier, "Pelvic Fractures and Pregnancy," *Journal of Trauma* 12, 6 (1972): 474-80.

James N. Glenn, Michael E. Miner, and Leonard F. Peltier, "The Treatment of Fractures of the Femur in Patients with Head Injuries," *Journal of Trauma* 13, 11 (1973): 958-61.

Frederick W. Reckling, Arlo S. Hermreck and Leonard F. Peltier, "The Trauma Conference: A Method of Teaching Management of the Injured Patient," *Journal of Trauma* 14, 10 (1974): 841-7.

Leonard F. Peltier, "Treatment of Trauma. The Fractured Pelvis," *Medical Times* 104, 1 (1976): 76-8.

Leonard F. Peltier, "The Diagnosis of Fractures of the Hip and Femur by Auscultatory Percussion," *Clinical Orthopaedics and Related Research* 123 (1977): 9-11.

R. R. Karpman, L. F. Peltier, C. Thies, and W. H. Fulcher, "Determination of Volume of Lower Extremities," *Surgical Forum* 30 (1979): 504-6.

Leonard F. Peltier, "A Capite ad Calcem: A Parable for Our Time," *Journal of Trauma* 21, 2 (1981): 96-8. (Presidential Address, American Association for the Surgery of Trauma 1980).

Andrew Macbeth, James Malone, Lawrence Norton and Leonard F. Peltier, "Paralysis and Aortic Thrombosis Following Blunt Abdominal Trauma," *Journal of Trauma* 22, 7 (1982): 591-4.

Leonard F. Peltier, "General Considerations of Fracture Treatment," "Injuries of the Upper Extremity," and "Injuries of the Lower Extremity," Chapters 20, 21, 22 in *Early Care of the Injured Patient*, ed. Alexander Walt for the Committee on Trauma of the American College of Surgeons (Philadelphia: W. B. Saunders, Co., 1982).

Leonard F. Peltier, *Fractures: A History and Iconography of Their Treatment* (San Francisco: Norman Publishing, 1990).

Leonard F. Peltier, "What We Have Learned From the Wars," *Instructional Course Lecture* 41 (1992): 487-91.

Leonard F. Peltier, "A Classic in Trauma Education," *Clinical Orthopaedics and Related Research* 339 (1997): 4-6.

Fat Embolism

"Whenever surgeons are confronted with patients suffering from injuries, especially fractures of the long bones, the possibility of fat embolism as a complication of the injury must be considered as a very real hazard."[1]
— LEONARD F. PELTIER, M.D., PH.D.

*F*at embolism is a defined clinical entity that can be a lethal complication after fractures of the long bones, pelvis and ribs. It also occasionally occurs after blunt trauma to the abdomen, and orthopedic operative procedures. It is a consequence of fat embolization, a condition in which fat globules large enough to occlude small blood vessels are released by damaged bone or soft tissue into the circulating blood.[2,3] Fat embolism should be suspected when injured patients exhibit rapid, shallow breathing and changes in the normal state of consciousness such as disorientation, delirium, confusion, or coma. The appearance of a petechial rash, especially over the upper torso, axillae, soft palate and in the conjunctiva, in the presence of pulmonary and cerebral symptoms, is strongly supportive of a fat embolism diagnosis. However, the rash doesn't always appear, and it may be transient and easily missed. The signs and symptoms of fat embolism may occur immediately after injury (mechanical phase), or there may be a delay of up to forty-eight hours (latent phase) before they appear during the chemical phase.

Understanding the pathophysiology of fat embolism, as well as identifying and developing techniques for its early diagnosis and treatment, became a major research focus for LFP early in his career.

He first became aware of the entity while he was stationed in Germany after World War II. "In 1947 I encountered my first case of a patient with fat embolism, a GI who had fractured both femurs in a Jeep accident. He developed petechiae, was out of his head, and was very sick. I didn't know what it was and someone told me it was fat embolism." LFP's next experience with fat embolism occurred near the end of his orthopedic residency at the University of Minnesota. "Then, in Minnesota, another severely injured patient seemed to be OK in the morning and died in the afternoon. I discovered there was no cure or understanding of fat embolism. It was a good thing to look into because no one knew [much] about it and you could [quickly] become an expert."

LFP began his study with a search of the medical literature and discovered that fat embolism had been documented in patients as early as 1913, when Warthin concluded that fat embolism was the most frequent cause of death after fractures of the long bones.[4,5] During World War I Sutton[6] estimated that 10% of the wounded passing through his casualty clearing station suffered from fat embolism. Later, during World War II and the Korean War, autopsy studies revealed that fat embolism was the cause of death in an alarming number of patients with fractures and blunt abdominal injuries.[7,8,9] Similar data were obtained from trauma in civilian life.

However, some physicians denied, or strongly questioned, the existence of fat embolism. Robert Whitson, in a 1951 article in the *Journal of Bone and Joint Surgery*, concluded that because there was no "convincing evidence in favor of the theory of fat embolism, …the diagnosis of fat embolism as a cause of death should be discontinued in favor of anoxyaemia [oxygen deficiency in the circulating blood]….The persistence of the concept of fat embolism has been a hindrance to the understanding and treatment of certain post-traumatic complications."[10] Edwin F. Cave, M.D., an orthopedic surgeon at the Massachusetts General Hospital in Boston, questioned the reality of the concept in his 1958 textbook, *Fractures and Other Injuries*.[11] Dr. Cave commented that although "an occasional case of the phenomenon continues to be observed from time to time, …it must be admitted that the significance of fat embolism in shock is still [in question]. No practical measures are known which can be taken against its occurrence—if, indeed, it is a reality."[12] At the time LFP initiated his research, Whitson's and Cave's opinions were prevalent.

Other reasons that the existence of fat embolism was disputed were that physicians may not have observed the patient at the actual time the petechiae were visible, and the exhibited mental confusion (actually due to oxygen deficiency from fat embolism damage to the lungs) was attributed to head trauma. In the 1950s, analyzing arterial blood oxygen levels was far more difficult than it is currently; thus, the serious oxygen deficiency was not easily identified.

Interestingly, anesthesiologists were often the ones to first suspect fat embolism when they noticed petechiae as they were preparing patients for cranial surgery. Before the development of diagnostic technology such as computerized tomography and magnetic resonance imaging to better identify brain damage, patients were often taken to the operating room for treatment when head injuries and increased intracranial pressure were suspected to be the source of disorientation and mental confusion. At this time anesthesiologists would sometimes notice petechiae on the patient's chest as they were starting intravenous infusions and applying monitoring pads. Their observations added credibility to the idea that fat embolism did exist.

Another fact that led some physicians to doubt the existence of the entity was that fat embolism was rarely diagnosed on pathology reports from autopsies. Frozen sections of tissue were required to find the fat droplets, and they were not routinely performed unless specifically requested. Furthermore, the stains normally used in preparation of tissue slides from autopsies actually dissolve the fat globules that would be diagnostic in fat embolism. Thus, the diagnosis was never accidentally "stumbled upon" by an unsuspecting pathologist.

The opinions of skeptics did not deter LFP from trying to study and understand the phenomenon. "The first big question was, where does the fat come from? [Some investigators] thought the fat was mobilized metabolically [as a response to the stress of an injury]. I thought the fat droplets came from the bone marrow."

With funds provided by the Markle Scholarship and grants from the Graduate School of the University of Minnesota, LFP began his investigation. Using two groups of mongrel dogs (seven dogs in one group, eight in the other), he studied the prophylactic value of a tourniquet in preventing embolization of fat droplets in the circulating blood.[13] In one group, the anesthetized dogs had each of their legs fractured with tourniquets applied to each extremity above the fracture before the procedure was carried out. The other group underwent the same treatment, but without tourniquets in place. In the group without tourniquets, five of the seven animals had fat droplets detected in the circulating blood within thirty minutes after fracturing the first limb. This finding was confirmed by appropriately stained sections of the lung, brain, and kidney at autopsy. In the group with tourniquets, no fat droplets could be detected until the tourniquets were removed ninety minutes later. As part of the same study, LFP conducted a study of 100 patients undergoing elective orthopedic operations that required drilling, cutting and/or manipulation of bone segments, with tourniquets employed above the operative site in forty-five of those patients. The results demonstrated that tourniquet application effectively sequestered fat distally in the operated extremity, exerting a positive prophylactic value in minimizing the degree of fat embolization.

Following these studies, LFP also documented the large amount of fat contained in human long bones,[14] as well as potential toxic properties of neutral fat and its metabolites, free fatty acids.[15] The striking finding from this latter study, in which rabbits were used, was that free fatty acids are much more toxic than oils and neutral fats. Postmortem examination of the rabbit tissues, as well as clinical findings after the injections, confirmed the toxicity of fatty acids on tissues such as lungs. While conducting his laboratory studies, LFP remained abreast of a developing body of literature reporting instances of fat embolism in injured humans. With this information, and continued further investigative studies, over time he was able to elucidate a theory of the pathophysiology of the clinical fat embolism syndrome, make some suggestions about prevention, and establish treatment interventions to attempt to prevent fatal outcomes.

LFP published his first journal article on fat embolism in 1952 and continued publishing his investigations. In 1957 his research on fat embolism won the coveted Kappa Delta Award, a $1,000.00 stipend presented to LFP at the American Academy of Orthopaedic Surgeons (AAOS) meeting in Chicago in January 1957.[16] The Kappa Delta Research Fellowship was established by the Kappa Delta sorority to honor achievement in laboratory or clinical research related to the musculoskeletal system. According to Marshall R. Urist, M.D., the recipient of the first Kappa Delta Award in 1950, the prize "has become a most highly valued form of recognition in our profession."[17] It was initiated when members of the sorority realized that correcting

Presentation of Kappa Delta Award to LFP
January 28, 1957

∾

(L to R): Dr. William Green, President of the American Academy of Orthopaedic Surgeons; LFP; Elizabeth Banta Mueller, Kappa Delta's representative; Dr. Donald Slocum

Photo courtesy of the Peltier family

yesterday's defects was not the entire answer to solving tomorrow's problems, and further inquiry revealed, to their amazement, that no significant award existed for the encouragement of orthopedic research.[18] They turned to the AAOS for a panel of experts to select the recipients, and the tradition has been maintained. In the years since their inception, the Kappa Delta Awards have totaled more than one million dollars, with the organization currently awarding three annual $20,000 fellowships for orthopedic research. LFP echoed Dr. Urist's view when he commented that he considered the sorority's contribution in supporting research "a tremendous stimulus—much more valuable [over time] than an equal contribution for hospital beds or other local facilities."[19]

After LFP moved from Minneapolis to Kansas, the support of various grants, laboratory technicians, space, and equipment enabled him to continue his investigations related to various aspects of fat embolism. He involved residents and colleagues in his research, and they examined laboratory and physical findings in the disease entity. Fat globules and fatty acids in blood and urine, and physical findings such as petechiae and hypoxia, were subjects of study.

As word spread in the professional domain about his research, previously skeptical colleagues began to accept the credibility of his work. In 1958 one of his residents, Federico Adler, M.D., presented a paper on fat embolism at the Surgical Forum of an American College of Surgeons meeting. After his talk, a physician in the audience congratulated Dr. Adler on his excellent presentation, relating that he recently had a case of fat embolism at his hospital. After the meeting, someone asked Dr. Adler if he was aware of the identity of the man who had complimented him. It turned out to be Dr. Edwin Cave, who had questioned the existence of the syndrome in his recently published textbook![20]

Once the concept of fat embolization was accepted, dispute continued about its pathophysiology. Sevitt[21] found fat in the brain, and therefore assumed that it caused the mental confusion. However, LFP and colleagues[22] determined that only a very tiny amount of neutral fat went to the brain…that practically all of it was arrested in the lung.

Another important finding of LFP's investigation was that an absence or decrease in lung surfactant activity was identified as being a major contributor to alveolar collapse, thus contributing to severe hypoxia.[23]

Once LFP understood many of the pathophysiologic processes occurring in fat embolism and developed techniques to evaluate and measure its signs and symptoms, he and his research colleagues were able to develop and explore a variety of treatment protocols. By 1969 LFP was able to describe his concept of the pathophysiology and treatment of fat embolism in one of his most important publications on this problem.[24] His understanding of the pulmonary pathology and development of interventions to prevent fatal outcomes was, at least in part, due to his early Ph.D. work observing respiration in post-polio patients confined to iron lungs.

LFP's Concept of the Pathophysiology and Treatment of Fat Embolism

∾

LFP's concept of the pathophysiology and treatment of fat embolism, based on a professional lifetime of clinical and laboratory investigations, can be summarized by the following somewhat oversimplified flow diagrams. Although there is no effort to indicate which factors are the most important, they emphasize the fact that ultimately fat embolism is a pulmonary disease.

The initiating event is an injury, most commonly a fracture or fractures of bones (femurs, pelvis, tibiae) that contain large amounts of neutral fat in their marrows. The fat is intravasated into the injured veins that drain the hematoma surrounding the fracture(s). The neutral fat is carried by the circulation to the heart and then to the lungs, where it can cause mechanical obstruction of the pulmonary capillaries. Additionally, if the patient is in shock due to blood loss, there will be increased stress on the lung alveoli due to hypoperfusion.

If the patient survives the early mechanical effects of the blockage of the pulmonary vascular bed with droplets of neutral fat, several additional pathological events occur. The circulating free neutral fat leads to platelet aggregation with subsequent release of platelet amines, which are in turn toxic to the pulmonary alveoli. Within a few hours the neutral fat in the lungs is hydrolysed into glycerol and free fatty acids by a facultative enzyme (lipase) naturally occurring in the lung. The free fatty acids in turn combine with calcium ions found in the walls of the pulmonary alveoli and blood capillaries, resulting in injury to those structures and contributing to additional pulmonary dysfunction. When injury to the capillaries of the skin occur, petechiae are often found and are considered a supportive diagnostic finding. The petechiae are most often seen over the anterior chest wall, axillae, soft palate and in the conjunctival mucosa, especially within the lower eyelid. They tend to appear for a relatively short period of time, fade, and often reappear. To support the diagnosis of fat embolism the petechiae can sometimes be provoked by applying a tourniquet to the extremities.

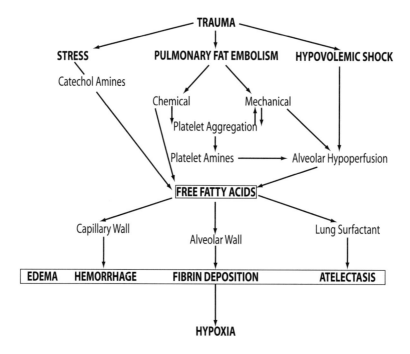

**LFP's Schematic Representation of the
Pathophysiology of Fat Embolism**

∾

*Drawing adapted by Carol Stevens from:
Peltier, L.F. "Fat Embolism, A Current Concept," Clinical Orthopaedics
and Related Research, 66 (Sept.-Oct. 1969): 247.*

Another toxic effect of free fatty acids is that they destroy lung surfactant. Lung surfactant is a substance normally present in the pulmonary alveoli. It keeps these "air sacs" open and distended by maintaining proper surface tension. When it is deficient or absent, the alveoli collapse, seriously compromising oxygen exchange. As a result of the complex sequence of actions and reactions to abnormal fat in the circulating blood, patients with fat embolism can develop severe, life-threatening pulmonary dysfunction. This pulmonary dysfunction results in hypoxemia, that in turn, produces cerebral symptoms such as confusion and disorientation.

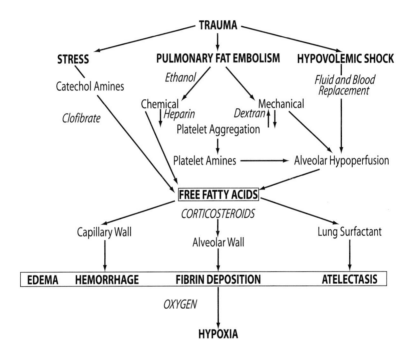

**Fat Embolism Treatment Interventions
Advocated by LFP**

∾

*Drawing adapted by Carol Stevens from:
Peltier, L.F. "Fat Embolism, A Current Concept," Clinical Orthopaedics
and Related Research, 66 (Sept.-Oct. 1969): 248.*

The prevention and treatment of fat embolism begins with careful immobilization of injured extremities (to prevent further release of fat globules from movement of the injured bones), correction of hypovolemia and support of respiration.

Adequate pulmonary perfusion must be accomplished, often requiring ventilatory support, the efficacy of which must be determined by monitoring blood gases. Corticosteroids, in their capacity to reduce the inflammatory reaction of the alveolar-capillary membranes to free fatty acids, as well as their protective effect on surfactant, have been found to be of help. A liter of intravenous alcohol (intravenous ethanol 5% and dextrose 5%), given over a twelve-hour period, was found to be helpful as a lipase inhibitor. The use of low-molecular-weight dextran, heparin and clofibrate as antihyperlipemic drugs were also advocated by some investigators, but LFP was not convinced of their efficacy.

During the next decade, in addition to his many other clinical, investigative, educational, and administrative responsibilities, LFP and various colleagues continued to study and refine diagnostic techniques and treatment protocols for fat embolism. For instance, in 1977 Stitt (KU '79) and Adler[25] were able to demonstrate that corticosteroid administration had a protective effect on lung surfactant activity, in addition to its previously identified capacity to reduce the inflammatory reaction of the alveolar-capillary membranes to free fatty acids. LFP continued to educate the medical community-at-large to be alert for the possibility of the existence of fat embolism after serious injuries. His scientific curiosity and willingness to plunge ahead, in spite of skeptics within his profession, provided the basis for understanding a phenomenon that continues to confront today's physicians. A recent literature search revealed no fewer than 352 scientific articles published in the recent ten-year period between 1993 and 2003 discussing the occurrence, pathophysiology, research, and treatment of fat embolism.

Notes and Sources

∾

1. Leonard F. Peltier, "The Classic: Fat Embolism, An Appraisal of the Problem," *Clinical Orthopaedics and Related Research* 187 (1984): 5.

2. Federico Adler, M.D., "Fat Embolism Versus Fat Embolization Following Total Hip Arthroplasty" [letter], *Journal of Bone and Joint Surgery* 85-A, 3 (2003): 569.

3. Leonard F. Peltier, M.D. "Fat Embolism," *Orthopedic Clinics of North America* 1, 1 (1970): 13.

4. Leonard F. Peltier, "An Appraisal of the Problem of Fat Embolism," *International Abstracts of Surgery* 104 (1957): 313-24 (Kappa Delta Award Essay).

5. A. S. Warthin, "Traumatic Lipemia and Fatty Embolism," *Int. Clin.* 4 (1913): 171.

6. G. E. Sutton, "Pulmonary Fat Embolism and Its Relation to Traumatic Shock," *British Medical Journal* 2 (1918): 368.

7. T. B. Mallory et al., "The General Pathology of Traumatic Shock," *Surgery* 27 (1950): 629.

8. R. T. Grant and E. B. Reeve, "Observations on the General Effects of Injury in Man," *Medical Research Council*, Special Report Series No. 277 (1951), London.

9. "Fat Embolism," *Annual Publication Historical Report*, 406th Medical General Laboratory, Professional Section (1951), Tokyo.

10. R. O. Whitson, "A Critique of Fat Embolism," *Journal of Bone and Joint Surgery* 33-A (1951): 447-50.

11. Edwin F. Cave, *Fractures and Other Injuries* (Chicago: Yearbook Publishers, 1958).

12. Ibid., p. 121.

13. Leonard F. Peltier, "Fat Embolism: The Prophylactic Value of a Tourniquet," *Journal of Bone and Joint Surgery* 38-A (1956): 835-40.

14. Leonard F. Peltier, "Fat Embolism: I. The Amount of Fat in Human Long Bones," *Surgery* 40 (1956): 657-60.

15. Leonard F. Peltier, "Fat Embolism: III. The Toxic Properties of Neutral Fat and Free Fatty Acids," *Surgery* 40 (1956): 665-70.

16. Elizabeth Banta Mueller, "Dr. Peltier Recipient of Kappa Delta's Orthopaedic Award," *The Angelos of Kappa Delta* (March, 1957): 243.

17. Esther Shauer Frear, "Ten for Ten Thousand," *The Angelos of Kappa Delta* (March, 1960): 196.

18. Ibid., 197.

19. Ibid., 198.

20. Federico Adler, M.D. (KU '60), telephone interview by JGL, December 20, 1999.

21. Simon Sevitt, *Fat Embolism* (London: Butterworth & Co., 1962).

22. S. Paredes, F. Comer, S. Rubin, Federico Adler and Leonard F. Peltier, "Fat Embolism; Distribution of Fat Tagged with I-131 Within the Body of the Rat At Various Times Following Intravenous Injection," *Journal of Bone and Joint Surgery* 47-A (1965): 1216-20.

23. R. W. Hamilton, Jr., R. F. Hustead and Leonard F. Peltier, "Fat Embolism: The Effect of Particulate Embolism on Lung Surfactant," *Surgery* 56 (1964): 53-6. Lung surfactant, tentatively identified in this study as dipalmityl lecithin, is responsible for low surface tension at the air-fluid interface, allowing the alveoli to remain expanded. At the time of this study, the absence of surfactant had been shown to play a critical role in some respiratory diseases of the neonatal period (atelectasis and hyaline membrane disease), but it had not been demonstrated as a problem in any adult disease process.

24. Leonard F. Peltier, "Fat Embolism: A Current Concept," *Clinical Orthopaedics and Related Research* 66 (1969): 241-53.

25. Ronald W. Stitt and Federico Adler, "Effect of Corticosteroids on Lung Surfactant Activity in Experimentally Produced Fat Embolism in Rats," *Surgical Forum* 28 (1977): 491-2.

Fat Embolism Publications

Leonard F. Peltier, "Fat Embolism Following Intramedullary Nailing: Report of a Fatality," *Surgery* 32 (1952): 719-22.

Leonard F. Peltier, "The Demonstration of Fat Embolism Tissue Sections Using Phosphin 3R, a Water Soluble Fluorochrome," *Journal of Laboratory and Clinical Medicine* 43 (1954): 321-3.

Leonard F. Peltier, "Fat Embolism: The Detection of Fat Emboli in the Circulating Blood," *Surgery* 36 (1954): 198-203.

Leonard F. Peltier, "The Use of Phosphin 3R, a Water-Soluble Fluorochrome in the Diagnosis of Fat Embolism," *Surgical Forum* 4 (1954): 176-8.

Leonard F. Peltier, "Fat Embolism: The Failure of Lipemia to Potentiate the Degree of Fat Embolism Accompanying Fractures of the Femur in Rabbits," *Surgery* 38 (1955): 720-2.

Leonard F. Peltier, "Fat Embolism: The Prophylactic Value of a Tourniquet," *Journal of Bone and Joint Surgery* 38-A (1956): 835-40.

Leonard F. Peltier, "Fat Embolism I: The Amount of Fat in Human Long Bones," *Surgery* 40 (1956): 657-60.

Leonard F. Peltier, Donald H. Wheeler, Harold M. Boyd and Joan Randolph Scott, "Fat Embolism: II. The Chemical Composition of Fat Obtained from Human Long Bones and Subcutaneous Tissue," *Surgery* 40 (1956): 661-4.

Leonard F. Peltier, "Fat Embolism: III. The Toxic Properties of Neutral Fat and Free Fatty Acids," *Surgery* 40 (1956): 665-70.

Leonard F. Peltier, "An Appraisal of the Problem of Fat Embolism," *International Abstracts of Surgery* 104 (1957): 313-24 (Kappa Delta Award Essay).

Leonard F. Peltier and Joan Randolph Scott, "Fat Embolism: Changes in the Level of Blood Lipase Following the Intravenous Injection of Neutral Fat, Fatty Acids and Other Substances into Dogs," *Surgery* 42 (1957): 541-7.

Leonard F. Peltier and Sing-Ping Lai, "Fat Embolism: Changes in the Serum Lipase Levels of Patients After Fresh Fractures and Orthopedic Operations," *Surgical Forum* 9 (1959): 748-51.

Federico Adler, Leonard F. Peltier and Sing-Ping Lai, "Fat Embolism: The Correlation of Serum Lipase Levels with the Incidence of Lipuria," *Surgical Forum* 10 (1959): 804-7.

Federico Adler, Leonard F. Peltier and Sing-Ping Lai, "Fat Embolism: The Determination of Fat in the Urine by Microscopic and Macroscopic Methods," *Surgery* 47 (1960): 959-61.

F. Price Cossman, Federico Adler, C. Frederick Kittle and Leonard F. Peltier, "Lipuria and Lipasemia After Thoracic Surgical Procedures," *Journal of Thoracic Surgery* 40 (1960): 430-41.

Leonard F. Peltier, Federico Adler and Sing-Ping Lai, "Fat Embolism: The Significance of an Elevated Serum Lipase After Trauma to Bone," *American Journal of Surgery* 99 (1960): 821-6.

Federico Adler, Sing-Ping Lai and Leonard F. Peltier, "Fat Embolism: Prophylactic Treatment with Lipase Inhibitors," *Surgical Forum* 12 (1961): 453-5.

Federico Adler and Leonard F. Peltier, "The Laboratory Diagnosis of Fat Embolism," *Clinical Orthopaedics and Related Research* 21 (1961): 226-31.

O. E. Aufranc, W. N. Jones and W. H. Harris, "Fracture of the Month, Number 1: Fat Emboli," Guest discussor, Leonard F. Peltier, *Journal of the American Medical Association* 178 (1961): 1187-90.

John L. Davies and Leonard F. Peltier, "Deep Ether Anesthesia and Fat Embolism," *Archives of Surgery* 82 (1961): 417-9.

Federico Adler and Leonard F. Peltier, "The Effect of Sublingual Potassium Heparin (Clarin) on the Serum Lipase Activity of Patients Following Fractures," *Journal of Trauma* 4 (1964): 390-3.

R. W. Hamilton, Jr., R. F. Hustead and Leonard F. Peltier, "Fat Embolism: The Effect of Particulate Embolism on Lung Surfactant," *Surgery* 56 (1964): 53-6.

Marian Kuenzig, Robert W. Hamilton, Jr., and Leonard F. Peltier, "Dipalmitoyl Lecithin: Studies on Surface Properties," *Journal of Applied Physiology* 20 (1965): 779-82.

S. Paredes, F. Comer, S. Rubins, Federico Adler and Leonard F. Peltier, "Fat Embolism; Distribution of Fat Tagged with I-131 Within the Body of the Rat At Various Times Following Intravenous Injection," *Journal of Bone and Joint Surgery* 47-A (1965): 1216-20.

Leonard F. Peltier, "The Diagnosis of Fat Embolism," *Surgery, Gynecology and Obstetrics* 121 (1965): 371-9.

Leonard F. Peltier, "Fat Embolism," *The Heart Bulletin* 14 (1965): 72-5.

James A. Evans, Robert W. Hamilton Jr., Marian C. Kuenzig and Leonard F. Peltier, "Effects of Anesthetic Agents on Surface Properties of Dipalmitoyl Lecithin: Lung Surfactant Model," *Anesthesia and Analgesia* 45 (1966): 285-9.

Leonard F. Peltier, "Fat Embolism," *Journal of the Louisiana State Medical Society* 118 (1966): 447-9.

H. James Armstrong, Marian C. Kuenzig and Leonard F. Peltier, "Lung Lipase Levels in Normal Rats and Rats with Experimentally Produced Fat Embolism," *Proceedings of the Society for Experimental Biology and Medicine* 124 (1967): 959-61.

James H. Garner, Jr. and Leonard F. Peltier, "Fat Embolism: The Significance of Provoked Petechiae," *Journal of the American Medical Association* 200 (1967): 556-7.

Leonard F. Peltier, "Fat Embolism: A Pulmonary Disease," *Surgery* 62 (1967): 756-8.

Leonard F. Peltier, "A Few Remarks on Fat Embolism," *Journal of Trauma* 8 (1968): 812-20.

John J. Wertzberger and Leonard F. Peltier, "Fat Embolism: The Importance of Arterial Hypoxia," *Surgery* 63 (1968): 626-9.

John J. Wertzberger and Leonard F. Peltier, "Fat Embolism: The Effect of Corticosteroids on Experimental Fat Embolism in the Rat," *Surgery* 64 (1968): 143-7.

Phillip L. Baker, Marian C. Kuenzig and Leonard F. Peltier, "Experimental Fat Embolism in Dogs," *Journal of Trauma* 9 (1969): 577-86.

Leonard F. Peltier, "Fat Embolism: A Current Concept," *Clinical Orthopaedics and Related Research* 66 (1969): 241-53.

Leonard F. Peltier, "Questions and Answers: Management of Pulmonary Fat Embolism in Vietnam Fracture Casualties," *Journal of the American Medical Association* 208 (1969): 2167.

Leonard F. Peltier, "Fat Embolism," *Orthopedic Clinics of North America* 1 (1970): 13-20.

Leonard F. Peltier, Chairman; Simon Sevitt, Rapporteur, "Trauma Workshop: Fat Embolism," *Journal of Trauma* 10 (1970): 1074-7.

Phillip L. Baker, James H. Kantor, Marian C. Kuenzig and Leonard F. Peltier, "Ethyl-2-(p-chlorophenoxy)-2methylproprionate (Clofibrate) in Experimental Fat Embolism in Rats," *Proceedings of the Society for Experimental Biology and Medicine* 136 (1971): 64-5.

Phillip L. Baker, Marian C. Kuenzig and Leonard F. Peltier, "Pulmonary Lymph in Experimental Fat Embolism," *Surgery* 69 (1971): 686-91.

Phillip L. Baker, John A. Pazell and Leonard F. Peltier, "Free Fatty Acids, Catecholamines and Arterial Hypoxia in Patients with Fat Embolism," *Journal of Trauma* 11 (1971): 1026-30.

Leonard F. Peltier, "The Diagnosis and Treatment of Fat Embolism," *Journal of Trauma* 11 (1971): 661-7.

Fat Embolism: Diagnosis and Treatment (supported by the Craig Foster Memorial Fund), exhibited at the Clinical Congress of the American College of Surgeons in Atlantic City in 1971, and the American Academy of Orthopaedic Surgeons annual meeting in Washington, D.C., in 1972.

John A. Pazell and Leonard F. Peltier, "Experience with Sixty-three Patients with Fat Embolism," *Surgery, Gynecology and Obstetrics* 135 (1972): 77-80.

Leonard F. Peltier, "Current Concepts. Clinical Diagnosis and Treatment of Fat Embolism," *Journal of the Kansas Medical Society* 75 (1974): 289-92.

Leonard F. Peltier, John A. Collins, Charles M. Evarts and Simon Sevitt, "A Panel by Correspondence: Fat Embolism," *Archives of Surgery* 109 (1974): 12-6.

Tape Slide Lecture, *Fat Embolism*, American Academy of Orthopaedic Surgeons, 1975.

Leonard F. Peltier, "Fat Embolism," in *Principles and Practice of Emergency Medicine,* ed. George B. Schwartz, Peter Safar, John H. Stone, Patrick B. Storey and David K. Wagner, (Vol. I, Philadelphia: W. B. Saunders Co., 1978): 786-90.

Leonard F. Peltier, "The Classic: Fat Embolism: An Appraisal of the Problem," *Clinical Orthopaedics and Related Research* 187 (1984): 3-17. (A reprinting of his 1957 Kappa Delta Award paper as a classic article).

Leonard F. Peltier, "Fat Embolism," in *Current Emergency Therapy*, ed. Richard F. Edlich and Daniel Spyker (Rockville, Maryland: Aspen Publication, 1985): 216-9.

Leonard F. Peltier, "Fat Embolism. A Perspective," *Clinical Orthopaedics and Related Research* 232 (1988): 263-70.

Plaster of Paris

"We were skeptical when we first heard the suggestion that plaster of Paris[1] could be used to fill defects and cavities in bones."

— LEONARD F. PELTIER, M.D., PH.D.

*F*ractures that are slow to heal and defects in bone caused by infection and benign conditions, such as bone cysts, make bone weak and vulnerable to failure. Treatment often requires addition of an auxiliary material to facilitate bone healing and repair. Healthy bone, in the form of a bone graft, for use in repair of such fractures and bony defects could be difficult to obtain in the 1950s. The tissue of choice, "the gold standard," was, and remains, bone from another site on the patient's own body (autologous bone graft, or autograft). However, the large amount of bone often needed for a graft and the limited amount of bone available from donor site(s) can make this solution impractical or ill-advised.[2] Additionally, the operation(s) necessary for obtaining bone is(are) not without documented potential complications, including hemorrhage, nerve injury, infection, chronic donor site pain and even herniation of abdominal viscera through the bony defect created in the most commonly used donor site, the ilium (referred to in lay terms as the hip bone).

In the 1950s human donor bone (allograft) from a bone bank was scarce and expensive. The first bone bank in the United States was established in 1949,[3] and although bone preservation techniques were evolving, donor bone from a bone bank in those years presented risk to the recipient. Safe storage of the tissue and maintenance of sterility were challenging, and prevention of disease transmission from the donor to the recipient could not be assured.

LFP read a 1953 article written in German by Kovacevic,[4] describing the use of plaster of Paris in three patients with osteomyelitis. Kovacevic removed the entire shaft of the infected tibia and replaced it with cylinders of plaster of Paris to which penicillin and sulfonamide powder had been added. Healing, with reconstitution of bone to fill the defect, occurred in each case. LFP found the report hard to believe. A wider review of the medical literature revealed scattered reports of the use of plaster of Paris to fill defects in experimental animals, and clinically in humans, with some success. The earliest report came from Trendelenburg's clinic in Bonn, Germany, in 1892.[5] The material was used in six patients to fill bone cavities resulting from tuberculosis, and in three of these patients it was reported that the cavities filled in solidly with new bone. However, there were no well-controlled large studies to document these reports, and details about the procedure were sketchy.[6] LFP talked about it with Dr. Wangensteen, and although at first they were skeptical, they decided that further investigation in the laboratory would be worthwhile. "Documentation [of the successful use of plaster of Paris] was just too plentiful to be brushed aside...I had my own research laboratory, funds, and [experimental] animals, ...and we embarked upon a series of [studies]."

LFP's initial plaster of Paris research was funded by a grant from the Graduate School of the University of Minnesota and a U.S. Public Health Service grant. In his early studies he prepared his own plaster of Paris materials (columns or pellets) by pouring the liquid material into aluminum foil molds. He then sterilized them with dry heat. Later he was able to obtain sterile plaster of Paris pellets, produced at his request by Ethicon Laboratories. These pellets were sterilized by a beam of ionizing irradiation.

LFP first studied the use of plaster of Paris pellets in promoting healing of large defects in animals (mongrel dogs). He examined the use of plaster of Paris materials alone, as well as plaster of Paris combined

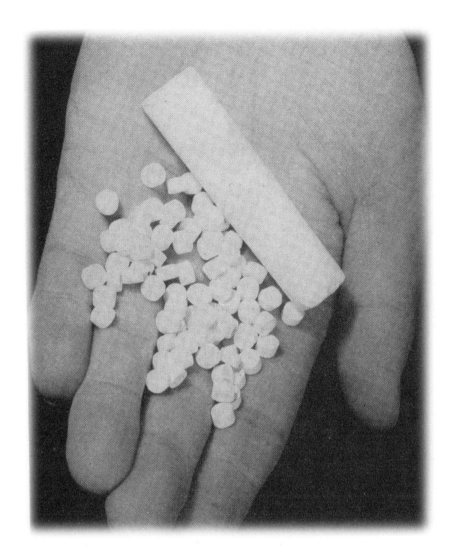

**A Handful of LFP's Plaster of Paris Pellet
and a Plaster of Paris Column**

∽

*Reprinted with permission of Lippincott, Williams & Wilkins from
L.F. Peltier et. al., "The Use of Plaster of Paris to Fill Defects in Bone,"
Annals of Surgery 146, 1 (July 1957): 61.*

with bone grafts (obtained from the bony material he removed to create
the defects). He compared autografts (bone grafts from the same animal)
and allografts (from another animal of the same species). In addition to
using invasive histological studies of the implanted bone grafts and
plaster of Paris to assess the healing process, LFP was able to use non-

invasive X-ray examinations, because plaster of Paris is a radiopaque material.

LFP concluded from these animal studies that 1) formed elements of plaster of Paris are easily sterilized and can be used to fill defects in bone; 2) plaster of Paris provides no internal support (it doesn't harden like a dried cast, but remains as a moist soft mass); 3) plaster of Paris is completely reabsorbed from the site of implantation after a period of weeks or months, and in the case of infection the plaster of Paris can drain out in the pus and does not remain as a foreign body; 4) the presence of plaster of Paris neither stimulates nor inhibits the normal growth of new bone; and 5) during the absorption of plaster of Paris in the dog, there may be a transient elevation of calcium in the circulating blood, but it is not harmful.[7] He also noted that fresh autografts were superior to fresh allografts. The addition of plaster of Paris to autografts did not appear to either promote or inhibit survival of the graft or regeneration of new bone. The addition of plaster of Paris to allografts resulted in a slightly larger number of successes than when allografts alone were used, but it was doubtful if these variations were significant.

Once convinced of the safety of the procedure, LFP began clinical studies in humans in November 1956. One of LFP's first patients was a three-year-old girl with a large benign bone cyst. Obtaining an autograft from her tiny body would have been destructive, if not impossible. The bone cyst, its contents and membrane were removed by thorough curettage, and the defect was packed with plaster of Paris pellets. LFP recalled that "the plaster of Paris technique was successful" in healing the defect resulting from removal of the cyst.

LFP continued his clinical research on plaster of Paris when he moved to the University of Kansas, and by 1960 he had collected a series of twenty patients in whom the material had been used to treat a variety of bone defects. In thirteen of those twenty patients[8] the bone defects healed without incident. Three of the remaining seven patients experienced drainage, but the bone defects healed eventually. In two patients there was either incomplete obliteration or no effect on bone cysts, and two others (one with fibrous dysplasia and one with a giant cell tumor) had recurrence of the original defect. LFP's conclusions from this clinical research in humans mirrored those he found in the animal studies, that the implantation of plaster of Paris in a defect in bone is safe and feasible for both infected and non-infected bones, and that its absorption, followed by reconstitution of the bone, occurs.

In 1961 LFP received the Nicolas Andry[9] Award for outstanding orthopedic research based on his laboratory and clinical investigations. "I was the recipient of the initial Nicolas Andry Award given by the Association of Bone and Joint Surgeons."[10] When Dr. Fred Thompson from New York City called to inform LFP of the honor, he and Marian were away from home, and Dr. Thompson relayed the message to their babysitter. The award was presented at a meeting in Mexico City and Acapulco, where LFP was requested to present his research. The Peltiers used the Andry monetary award for Marian's travel expenses. According to LFP, "A lineal descendent of the 4th Viceroy[11] of Mexico coordinated the program. [While in Mexico] we traveled by bus to Acapulco and it was a memorable experience."

In 1978[12] LFP reported on the use of plaster of Paris pellets in the treatment of patients with unicameral bone cysts (benign, single-chambered cystic lesions predominately seen in the first two decades of life and subject to pathological fracture). This series included twenty-six consecutive patients from Minnesota, Kansas and Arizona, ranging in age from two to fourteen years with a follow-up of from one to twenty years. Sites of the cysts included the humerus (17), femur (6), radius (2), and calcaneus (1). All of the patients were treated by curettage of the cyst, followed by packing of the cavity with plaster of Paris pellets. Twenty-two patients went on to heal without incident. Two required a second operation because of drainage and recurrence of the cysts, another required wound debridement for an infection, but went on to heal, and a fourth experienced a partial recurrence of the cyst, but did not require reoperation. These results compare very favorably with results reported on other methods of treatment.[13]

LFP continued to use and study plaster of Paris (calcium sulfate) in his patients. In 1981, with two colleagues at Arizona, Donald P. Speer, M.D., and Milos Chvapil, M.D., Ph.D., he published a paper entitled "Synthetic Bone Graft for Clinical Use: Comparison of Calcium Sulfate

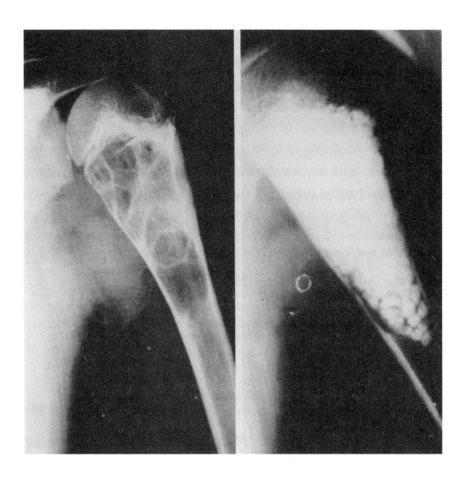

Fig. 1-A   Fig. 1-B
Roentgenograms of the Humerus —
∾
Fig. 1-A: Large cyst of the humerus
Fig. 1-B: Cyst filled with plaster of Paris pellets

and Collagen Sponge."[14] In 1992 LFP co-authored, with Dr. Speer, a chapter entitled "Calcium Sulfate," in Habal and Reddi, *Bone Grafts and Bone Substitutes*[15] where they point out that calcium sulfate can be used to effectively extend (increase) the ultimate volume of autograft. It can be mixed with autograft, collagen fibers, and hydroxyapatite crystals without affecting the properties of the other materials. Furthermore, it can function as a vehicle for many agents such as antimicrobials, antibiotics and other drugs.

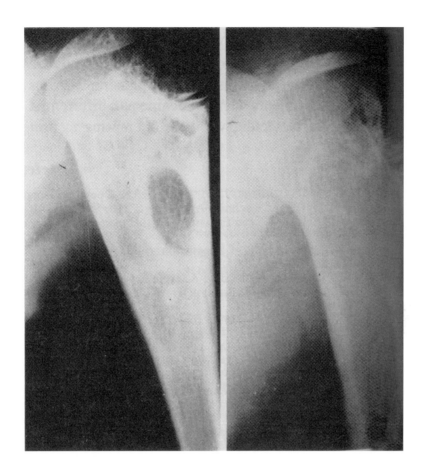

Fig. 1-C   Fig. 1-D
— of a Twelve-Year-Old Boy

∽

Fig. 1-C: One year after operation
Fig. 1-D: Three years after operation

Reprinted with permission of the JBJS from Leonard F. Peltier and Richard H. Jones, "Treatment of Unicameral Bone Cysts by Curettage and Packing with Plaster of Paris Pellets," Journal of Bone and Joint Surgery 60-A (1978): 820-2.

LFP's research and publications contributed to the marketing of plaster of Paris pellets for medical use in the United States. In 1996 the Food and Drug Administration approved the release of a surgical grade calcium sulfate named Osteoset (Wright Medical, Arlington, TN), provided in 4.8 mm and 3 mm diameter hard pellets.[16] In 1997 Wright Medical Technology introduced Osteoset at a reception at the annual meeting of the American Academy of Orthopaedic Surgeons. Osteoset is a safe, biocompatible, osteoconductive bone graft substitute that acts well as a space filler, preventing the ingrowth of soft tissue and thus allowing osseous ingrowth to occur in bony defects.[17]

Studies have shown that another very promising potential use of calcium sulfate is to deliver high concentrations of antibiotics directly to the site of bone infections, accomplished by packing infected bony defects with plaster of Paris impregnated with antibiotics.[18] This direct delivery alternative is desirable because treating infected bone with systemic (administered intravenously and affecting the entire body) antibiotics is not always effective. Due to impaired blood supply to the damaged bony tissue, antibiotic levels achieved in sequestered bone (a piece of dead bone that has become separated from, or is abnormally attached to, the surrounding healthy tissue) by systemic administration may be much lower than in the serum or the surrounding tissue. Furthermore, high levels of antibiotics delivered systemically can be toxic to some organ systems, and the mechanics of their delivery can result in complications associated with long-term intravenous access.

Currently an ongoing search for a more effective and less expensive method of delivering antibiotics to bony defects, avoiding undesirable consequences, is underway and includes the investigation of calcium sulfate as a vehicle. A form of antibiotic-laden plaster of Paris pellets (Osteoset-T, containing tobramycin) is now marketed in Europe and Canada, but as of late 2003 was not approved by the U.S. Food and Drug Administration for use in humans.[19]

Whatever the role that plaster of Paris (calcium sulfate) ultimately plays in the treatment regimens of bony defects, and as a bone graft extender, or as a local delivery system for antibiotics, it will be as a consequence and tribute to the pioneering efforts of LFP.

Notes and Sources

1. Plaster of Paris or gypsum (calcium sulfate dihydrate) is a fine powder, that, with the addition of water to create a porous mass, is used extensively in making casts and bandages to support or immobilize body parts, and in dentistry for taking dental impressions.

2. Leonard F. Peltier and Richard H. Jones, "Treatment of Unicameral Bone Cysts by Curettage and Packing with Plaster of Paris Pellets," *Journal of Bone and Joint Surgery (JBJS)* 60-A (1978): 820-2.

3. The U.S. Navy established the first United States tissue bank at Bethesda, Maryland, in 1949, giving the nation its first bone and tissue processing facility. The Massachusetts General Hospital Bone Bank was founded in 1971. www.mgh.harvard.edu/ortho

   By 1986 there were more than 300 nonprofit bone banks in operation, although consolidation since has decreased that number by nearly half. In the late 1980s the federal Food and Drug Administration announced its intention to regulate tissue banking, and began this oversight in 1993. Additional regulations were announced in 1997, including the registration of all tissue processors. www.mdtransplant.org/tissue/history

4. B. Kovacevic, "Ein Beitrag zum Problem der hämatogenen Osteomyelitis," *Archiv fur Klinische Chirurgie* 276 (1953): 432.

5. H. Dreesman, "Ueber Knochenplombierung," *Beitr. klin. Chir.* 9 (1892): 804-10.

6. Leonard F. Peltier, "The Use of Plaster of Paris to Fill Defects in Bone," *Clinical Orthopaedics and Related Research* 21 (1961): 1-31. (Nicolas Andry Award Essay).

7. Ibid., p. 12.

8. Ibid., pp. 28-9.

9. See Kansas chapter for information regarding Nicolas Andry.

10. The Association of Bone and Joint Surgeons (ABJS) was conceived in 1947 by a group of orthopedic surgeons to give younger orthopedists a forum in which to present papers, publish manuscripts, and share experiences with colleagues. Prior to its formation, there were limited programs and meetings and only one exclusive orthopedic journal, making competition extremely difficult for up and coming orthopedists in a

rapidly growing specialty. The official publication of the ABJS is *Clinical Orthopaedics and Related Research*. www.abjs.org

11. The viceroy system was initiated at the time of Columbus when Antonio de Mendoza was appointed as the first viceroy of Mexico (then known as New Spain) in 1535. A viceroy (derived from the words vice and royal) is someone who governs a country or province as a substitute for the monarch. He was also sometimes referred to as the king's "alter ego." His wife is referred to as a *vicereine*. Over a period of three centuries, a total of 61 viceroys ruled over New Spain's regions, which included all of what is now Mexico, Central America down to the southern border of Costa Rica, California, Arizona, New Mexico, Texas and the Philippines, as well as other areas. The system established by Mendoza designated that a viceroy's term should be six years, but individuals often fulfilled more than one term. Thus, the second viceroy of Mexico, Luis de Velasco, served from 1550 to 1564. His son, with the same name as his father, was viceroy of Mexico twice (1590-5 and 1607-11). www.historicaltextarchive.com www.bartleby.com

12. Peltier and Jones, *JBJS* (1978).

13. E. H. Boseker, W. H. Bickel, and D. C. Dahlin, "A Clinicopathologic Study of Simple Unicameral Bone Cysts," *Surgery, Gynecology and Obstetrics* 127 (1968): 550-60.

14. Donald P. Speer, Leonard F. Peltier and Milos Chvapil, "Synthetic Bone Graft for Clinical Use: Comparison of Calcium Sulfate and Collagen Sponge," *Transactions of the Orthopaedic Research Society* 6 (1981): 111.

15. Leonard F. Peltier and Donald P. Speer, "Calcium Sulfate," chap. 22 in Mutaz B. Habal and A. Hari Reddi, *Bone Grafts and Bone Substitutes* (Philadelphia: W. B. Saunders Co., 1992).

16. Robert W. Bucholz, "Nonallograft Osteoconductive Bone Graft Substitutes," *Clinical Orthopaedics and Related Research* 395 (2002): 44-52. Osteoconduction refers to the ingrowth of new bone onto, and replacing, a previously existing structure or scaffold.

17. Ibid., p. 51.

18. T. Miclau, L. E. Dahners, R. W. Lindsey, "In vitro pharmacokinetics of antibiotic release from locally implantable materials," *Journal of Orthopaedic Research* 11, 5 (1993): 627-32.

19. Cary P. Hagan, Senior Director Biologics Marketing, Wright Medical Technology, Inc., personal communication to FWR, October 6, 2003.

Plaster of Paris Publications

❧

Leonard F. Peltier and Robert Lillo, "The Substitution of Plaster of Paris Rods for Portions of the Diaphysis of the Radius in Dogs," *Surgical Forum* 6 (1956): 556-8.

Leonard F. Peltier, Earl Y. Bickel, Robert Lillo and Maung Soe Thein, "The Use of Plaster of Paris to Fill Defects in Bone," *Annals of Surgery* 146 (1957): 61-9.

Leonard F. Peltier and Duane Orn, "The Effect of Addition of Plaster of Paris to Autogenous and Homogenous Bone Grafts in Dogs," *Surgical Forum* 8 (1958): 571-4.

Leonard F. Peltier, "The Use of Plaster of Paris to Fill Large Defects in Bones: A Preliminary Report," *American Journal of Surgery* 97 (1959): 311-5.

Leonard F. Peltier, "The Use of Plaster of Paris to Fill Defects in Bone," *Clinical Orthopaedics and Related Research* 21 (1961): 1-31. (Nicolas Andry Award Essay)

Leonard F. Peltier, and Richard H. Jones, "Treatment of Unicameral Bone Cysts by Curettage and Packing with Plaster of Paris Pellets," *Journal of Bone and Joint Surgery* 60-A (1978): 820-2.

Donald P. Speer, Leonard F. Peltier and Milos Chvapil, "Synthetic Bone Graft for Clinical Use: Comparison of Calcium Sulfate and Collagen Sponge," *Transactions of the Orthopaedic Research Society* 6 (1981): 111.

Leonard F. Peltier and Donald P. Speer, "Calcium Sulfate," chap. 22 in Mutaz B. Habal and A. Hari Reddi, *Bone Grafts and Bone Substitutes* (Philadelphia: W. B. Saunders Co., 1992).

Leonard F. Peltier, "The Use of Plaster of Paris to Fill Large Defects in Bone: a Preliminary Report. 1959," *Clinical Orthopaedics and Related Research* 382 (2001): 3-5.

The History of Medicine

*"He is the real medical historian for our time. His literary
knowledge of the masters of medical science places him
in a position of pre-eminence in the field."*
— MARSHALL R. URIST, M.D.[1]
EDITOR-IN-CHIEF
CLINICAL ORTHOPAEDICS AND RELATED RESEARCH

∽*T*he seed for LFP's fascination with history may well have been sown in
early childhood. With encouragement from his father, a long-time
academician, and his mother who was a librarian prior to her marriage,
LFP early on became a very intense, rapid reader with almost total
recall. He loved reading about a variety of historical topics but attributed
his specific interest in medical history to his mentor, Owen H.
Wangensteen, M.D., Ph.D., at the University of Minnesota. "It was
difficult to listen to Dr. Wangensteen in the operating room, on rounds,
or in his lectures without hearing some allusion to the history of surgery.
He spoke familiarly of the famous 19th century surgeons as if they were
his contemporaries and his personal friends." According to LFP, OHW
decided that the residents needed to learn medical history. To encourage
this facet of their education, OHW included in his teaching program
four historical presentations a year by the various residents. "I was the
first chosen to lecture and my assigned topic was Lister."[2]

Later, while preparing for the orthopedic board examinations, LFP
became interested in eponymic fractures.[3] He was aware that during
the oral exam, candidates were often asked questions such as "What is
a Barton's fracture and how should it be managed?" His orthopedic
chief, Dr. Wallace Cole, suggested that he go to the literature and look

up the original papers by Barton and others whose names have become associated with a particular fracture. LFP did so, found it fascinating, and subsequently (1953-72) published a number of articles on eponymic fractures in which he not only talked about the fractures and their treatment, but also about the times, social settings and personalities of those who created the initial descriptions, including: John Rhea Barton (Barton's Fracture), Abraham Colles (Colles' Fracture), Giovanni Battista Monteggia (Monteggia's Fracture), Guillaume Dupuytren (Dupuytren's Fracture), Joseph Francoise Malgaigne (Malgaigne's Fracture), Robert William Smith (Smith's Fracture), Percivall Pott (Pott's Fracture), Riccardo Galeazzi (Galeazzi's Fracture), and Robert Jones (Jones' Fracture).[4] Many of the original papers describing these fractures were written in French, Italian or German. LFP's ability to read them was, at least in part, due to the language requirements for a Ph.D. in OHW's surgery program.

As mentioned previously, during his years at Kansas LFP became well acquainted with Dr. Ralph Major, Professor Emeritus of Internal Medicine and former Director of the Clendening History of Medicine Library and Museum at the University of Kansas. His relationship with Dr. Major and the library's rare books collection enabled LFP to pursue his avid interest, investigation and writing in the history of medicine arena. Upon his death, LFP willed his collection of approximately 1000 rare historical medical books along with a number of artifacts to the Clendening Library and Museum. The artifacts include a pewter bed pan, two pewter enema syringes, a bleeding bowl, a fleam (a sharp lancet used for blood-letting), two amputation saws, a WWI surgical set and a case with forceps, a WWII pouch containing bandages, an amputation kit in a wooden box, a leather medicine case, a blood count kit, and a WWII roll of surgical instruments.[5]

Clendening History of Medicine Library and Museum[6]

❧

The Clendening History of Medicine Library and Museum is the rare books and manuscripts library of the University of Kansas Medical Center. It actively collects rare books as well as current works in the history of medicine, nursing, and the allied health professions. It sponsors a "Digital Collection" on its web site. The library supports the biomedical ethics and medical humanities curriculum by collecting contemporary secondary works in these areas, and under the auspices of its museum, owns hundreds of medical artifacts.

Special collections include Florence Nightingale letters, the Paul Harrington (KU '35, KUMed '38) collection of spinal instrumentation artifacts, photographs, drawings and papers, Ralph Major photographs, and Rudolph Virchow manuscripts, as well as others.

Clendening Library was established in 1939 when Dorothy Hixon Clendening donated a laboratory building, Hixon Hall, to the University of Kansas Medical Center. One floor was devoted to a library, and the original collection of history of medicine works was donated by Logan Clendening at that time, as well as his collection of 6,000 volumes upon his death in 1945. The library has continued to acquire books through donation of important collections, as well as through direct purchase, and currently has more than 26,000 volumes.

The Clendening History of Medicine Library and Museum is one of three components of the KU History and Philosophy of Medicine Department. The other two include the Archives of KU Medical Center, as well as an Academic Department that offers formal courses and independent study in history and ethics. Three KU medical students over the years have won the national Osler Medal competition for the best essay in medical history. The Osler Medal is awarded by the American Association for the History of Medicine to a student in a school of medicine or osteopathy in the United States and Canada for the best unpublished essay in the history of medicine, naming a suitable recipient just fifty-five times over the last sixty-two years. KU ranks with top schools nationally in the number of Osler Medals awarded: Yale (8); McGill (6); Harvard (5); U. Penn (4), and KU and Johns Hopkins tied at (3).[7]

Logan Clendening, born in Kansas City, Missouri, and educated in the local public schools, the University of Michigan and the University of Kansas (M.D., 1907) was a most colorful figure. A tall, handsome man, straight but ample of girth, he exhibited an appearance of vigor, health and good spirits. After medical school he traveled, studied abroad and developed a passion for visiting the shrines of medical heroes. He began his private practice of medicine in Kansas City in 1914. In 1917 he was commissioned a major in the U.S. Army Medical Corps. When he returned from a two-year stint in the military, he resumed his private practice and was appointed instructor of medicine at the University of Kansas. He threw himself into the teaching of medical students, particularly physical diagnosis. He was fond of quoting Osler to the effect that many correct diagnoses were based on acute observation. "You recognize immediately what you have seen before." In 1924 he published his first medical work, *Methods of Treatment*. This book was filled with interesting bits of medical history, amusing anecdotes and sound common sense. It fell into the hands of the well-known American journalist and satirist, H. L. Mencken, who prevailed upon Clendening to write a medical book telling the American people just how their body organs were built and how they worked. The result was the instantly successful *The Human Body*. Subsequently Clendening was encouraged to write a daily newspaper column on health advice. This was very successful, and at the time of his death it appeared in 383 daily newspapers with a combined circulation of twenty-five million. Due to the demands

Logan Clendening, M.D.[8]
1884-1945

of writing, he withdrew from private practice but continued to teach physical diagnosis and see patients in the clinic at the University Hospital. With more leisure time and increased means, he was able to pursue his passion for medical history, and he soon assembled one of the finest private collections of old books in the country, becoming at once the despair and envy of his bibliophilic friends. Logan Clendening died in Kansas City on 31 January 1945.

Photo courtesy of University of Kansas Medical Center Archives
Department of History and Philosophy of Medicine

Ralph Major, born in Liberty, Missouri, obtained his A.B. from William Jewell College in 1902 and studied abroad in Leipzig, Munich and Heidelberg, Germany, before entering medical school at Johns Hopkins. After receiving his M.D., he returned to Europe to serve as an assistant in clinics, then returned to the U.S. in 1913 to study pathology at Stanford University. He joined the faculty of the University of Kansas (KU) School of Medicine in 1914 as Professor of Pathology. In 1919 he went to Detroit (Henry Ford Hospital) to train in internal medicine and returned as the first Chairman of a young, vigorous Department of Internal Medicine at KU in 1921, a position he retained until 1950. In 1923 he was among the first U.S. physicians to treat diabetics with insulin. From 1950 to 1954 he directed the History of Medicine department at the University of Kansas School of Medicine. He authored more than 200 articles and ten books, among which was his classic *Physical Diagnosis* textbook, first published in 1937 and translated into six languages. In his retirement years he traveled extensively and enlarged his valuable medical history collection that subsequently was added to the Clendening History of Medicine Library. Dr. Major died on 15 October 1970 at KU Medical Center in Kansas City.

Photo courtesy of University of Kansas Medical Center Archives Department of History and Philosophy of Medicine

Ralph H. Major, M.D.[9]
1884-1970
ᘯ

As did his mentor OHW, LFP shared his enthusiasm for the history of medicine with those around him and often incorporated historical anecdotes in his teaching. Throughout his life he frequented libraries in a variety of locations. At the University of Arizona Health Sciences Center he chaired the Library Advisory Committee for years (1973-90), and colleagues there admired and respected him. "Dr. Peltier's innate curiosity is contagious. His stories about the people who he was investigating made you want to find out more about them."[10] "I came to realize that he had a marvelous memory for detail and had learned as much about books and bibliography [through his informal study] as any librarian is taught during a year or so in library school."[11]

LFP occasionally celebrated historical events in his social life as well, and his memory lives on in those who shared his enthusiasm. "Every year on Bastille Day, July 14, my husband and I make a point to think of Dr. Peltier. He used to make an observance of sorts. I recall what was probably a tongue-in-cheek statement to the effect that with his French name and love of history, it was fitting to make a respectful bow to the liberation of the prison, wear the tricolor....Roy and I attended a lovely Bastille Day celebration one year, at least; he and Mrs. Peltier hosted it at their home. This delightful, small idiosyncracy brings a smile, even after all these years!"[12]

Through his writing efforts LFP attained national recognition as a medical historian. In 1977 he was invited to address the Clinical Congress of the American College of Surgeons in Dallas, Texas. His presentation, "John Jones: An Extraordinary American," was part of the opening ceremony. John Jones, born in Long Island in 1729 and educated in England and Europe, was a co-founder and professor of surgery at King's College in New York City. While serving in the Continental Army he wrote a small manual, addressed to U.S. military surgeons. This little volume has the distinction of being the first American medical book, the first American surgical monograph, the first American army manual, and the first American monograph dealing with public health and hygiene.[13, 14] Following the Revolutionary War, while Jones

JOHN JONES M.D.

~

Courtesy of the American College of Surgeons

was living in Philadelphia, both Benjamin Franklin and George Washington were among his patients.

In 1979 LFP was appointed Classics Editor for *Clinical Orthopaedics and Related Research (CORR)*, the official journal published by the Association of Bone and Joint Surgeons.[15] This was no small undertaking, as the Classics Editor is responsible for selecting a classic article for nearly every issue of the journal. When LFP accepted the responsibility at *CORR*, it was published six times a year. It became a monthly publication in 1985, doubling the number of classics articles per year that required selection and scholarly explanations.

Over its fifty years of existence *CORR* has maintained a two- or three-part format.[16] The first part is a symposium on a specific topic, the second features miscellaneous articles and current orthopedic topics, and the third, added in 1994, includes special features and Orthopaedic, Radiology, and Pathology Conferences. In most issues the classic article, a journal tradition over the years, introduces the symposium section of each edition, focusing on a topic pertinent to the subject matter of the symposium. The Classics Editor, in addition to selecting the article, writes a one- or two-paragraph biographical sketch of the author of the classic, obtains a photograph of that original author, and explains why the article was considered a classic.[17] LFP continued this responsibility for more than twenty years, until his death in May of 2003, contributing to more than 200 issues of the journal. Four issues containing his work were published posthumously, demonstrating his productivity right up to the end.[18]

The late Dr. Marshal Urist, *CORR*'s former Editor-in-Chief, commented regarding LFP's qualifications and contributions: "Very early in his illustrious career Peltier became enamored of the history of medicine, and since 1979 he has ably served as the Classics Editor of *Clinical Orthopaedics and Related Research*. Considering [that] the…roots of orthopedic surgery of the 20th century [are] in the general surgery of the 19th century, Leonard Peltier stands with one foot in each, serving as Classics Editor. He is the ideal historian for our time. His literary knowledge of the masters of medical science place him in a position of pre-eminence in the field."[19]

Carl T. Brighton, M.D., Ph.D.,[20] who followed Dr. Urist as Editor-in-Chief of *CORR* in 1993, remarked: "I have found [Dr. Peltier's] work to be invaluable to me because I certainly do not have the knowledge of history the way Dr. Peltier does and even if I had the knowledge of history, I would not know where to turn to find all the [pertinent] information. His contributions to *CORR* and to me personally are truly invaluable."[21] "Every week or two I would call Leonard by phone to discuss one or more Classic Articles for upcoming *CORR* issues. Frequently he would come up with an earlier article in the field that neither I, nor the Guest Editor for that particular symposium, knew about. When that happened, I would ask Leonard where in the world he found that article. He would always say something like, 'Oh, I have my sources' (he had a great, wry sense of humor). He also had his 'sources' for finding historical material on the author of each selected Classic Article. A most fruitful source was often the obituary in the Classic author's hometown newspaper!"[22]

According to Dr. Brighton: "Two recent examples of how Leonard could reach back in time in his mental file and pull out an article that truly captured the theme of a given monthly symposium are *CORR* symposia published in 2000, and 2003, respectively. For an 'Ethics in Orthopaedics' symposium,[23] Leonard selected as the Classic an excerpt that was taken from the novel 'Madam Bovary.'[24] In the story, Charles Bovary, a small town doctor in 19th century France, wanted to please his socially ambitious wife (Madam Bovary) by making a name for himself and thereby gain fame and fortune and perhaps move to Paris to reap the benefits of his newly-found celebrity status. He elected to treat the clubfoot of an active laborer. He devised a wooden box or mold into which he forced the deformed foot following an Achilles [heel cord] tenotomy. The tenotomy itself was a recently described procedure; Charles had never seen the procedure performed. Five days later, the patient was in grave pain. When the wooden box was removed, the foot was so gangrenous that a below-the-knee amputation had to be performed! In Leonard's biographical sketch of Flaubert, he sums up the purpose of the symposium by stating, 'Flaubert's novel poses ethical questions that are important for us to consider today...poor Hippolyte [the patient's name] was not the first patient nor the last, to be the victim of an ambitious surgeon.'[25]

"In late 2002, only a few months before LFP died, he selected the Classic article for a symposium entitled 'Injury Prevention.'[26] The original article, entitled, 'Football Injuries of the Harvard Squad for Three Years Under the Revised Rules,' was published in 1909.[27] In those days Harvard was one of the nation's football powerhouses, (!) but its team players had sustained so many injuries on the field that the President of Harvard banned the sport until it was made safer. In response to this, a uniform was designed. That picture alone is worth a thousand words on the state-of-the-art of injury prevention."[28]

Throughout his career LFP talked about writing a book on the history of the treatment of fractures. He began working on the project in 1984, and the book, with 270 illustrations and entitled *Fractures: A History and Iconography of Their Treatment*, was published by Norman Publishing, San Francisco, in 1990.

Reviews from across the medical spectrum were excellent: "This is an altogether admirable book, not least because it is written by a practicing surgeon who is also an academic and administrator of distinction and a scholar able to take both a wide and a long view of his subject. From an enormous literature, he has skillfully selected the cardinal accounts, illustrated, even from antiquity, by instantly illuminating

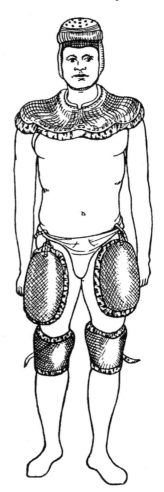

**Harvard Football Gear
Circa 1909**

∾

Edward H. Nichols, M.D., and Frank L. Richardson, M.D., "Football Injuries of the Harvard Squad for Three Years Under the Revised Rules," Boston Med. Surg. J. 160 (1909): 33-7.

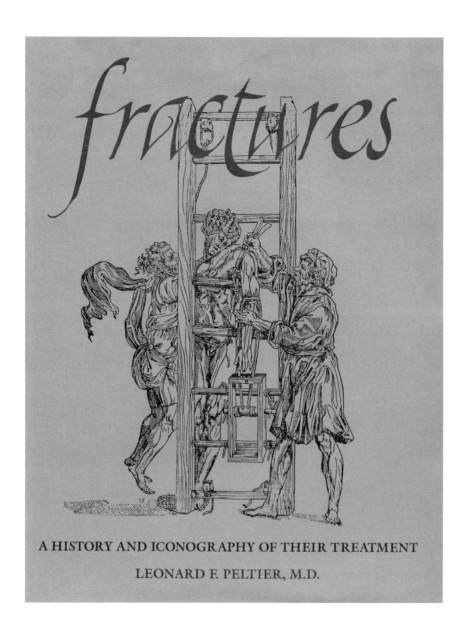

fractures

A HISTORY AND ICONOGRAPHY OF THEIR TREATMENT

LEONARD F. PELTIER, M.D.

Leonard F. Peltier, *Fractures: A History and Iconography of Their Treatment* (San Francisco: Norman Publishing, 1990)

∾

pictures...One is constantly reminded of the ingenuity of our predecessors. The study of history teaches those willing to learn, that we are not so clever as we think. Dr. Peltier has given this message fresh impetus, backed by authority based upon [universal] reading and much experience."[29] Another reviewer described "the first impression one conjures up while perusing this beautiful book is that this has to be a work of love by the author. This book cries out for the medical bibliophile. It is an extensive historical account of what is considered the most frequently suffered and commonly treated of all ailments...It truly is one of the most well-written, beautifully illustrated, and extensively referenced and researched texts on the subject of fractures."[30] A third reviewer proclaimed "This marvelous historical summary of fracture treatment from the time of pharaohs to nearly the present should be required reading for all orthopedic residents and for all surgeons who treat fractures. It updates the classic works of Malgaigne and Gurlt, published in the 19th century, and brings them up to just past the mid-20th century. It should be in the library of any serious student of fracture management. It will be enjoyed by anyone interested in the history of medicine."[31] And a fourth reminded the reader that "this book is of great value to the orthopaedist who is interested in 'firsts.' It is quite likely to humble those who believe that they have developed a 'new' way of management of an injury; they may well discover that a theory, principle, or practice regarded as unique is merely an application of a new technical detail, a product of the technical advances of this century."[32]

LFP wrote a companion volume to his fractures history, entitled *Orthopedics: A History and Iconography*, published in 1993, also by Norman Publishing in San Francisco.

This work traced the development of the specialty up to the time the book was written, focusing on the patient and disease, with 332 illustrations of patients, apparatus, X-rays, instruments, operative procedures and practitioners. It "...presents the history of various diseases and the corresponding physical appearance of the patient, interspersed with extensive use of the words of those who first described the conditions. This approach gives particular importance to the functional effects of conditions, such as poliomyelitis, not usually found in medical texts...The book has many virtues to recommend it to the reader, including the scholarship of the author."[33] "*Orthopedics: A History and Iconography* is a book that can satisfy two reading urges, enriching our professional knowledge as well as our cultural experience. Dr. Peltier takes readers through a spectrum of orthopedic pathology, starting in the days of the ancient Greeks and finishing with the present...In a clear writing style, the author [also] identifies pivotal events and extraordinary physicians and researchers who shaped the history of orthopedics."[34]

In 1994 LFP and his longtime friend and colleague, J. Bradley Aust, M.D., Ph.D., the Dr. Witten B. Russ Professor and Chairman of the Department of Surgery, University of Texas, San Antonio, completed a biography of their mentor, Dr. Owen H. Wangensteen. Dr. Aust recalls "I had occasion to be selected as the Surgical Alumnus of the Year at the University of Minnesota and gave a talk on Dr. Wangensteen's major contribution to the Surgical

Leonard F. Peltier, *Orthopedics: A History and Iconography* (San Francisco: Norman Publishing, 1993).

Forum as a component of the yearly meeting of the American College of Surgeons. This was published in a University of Minnesota bulletin, and John Lewis, M.D., who had been...one of Leonard's and my mentors in surgery at Minnesota, happened to write me and suggested that I should write the biography of Dr. Wangensteen. I mentioned this to Dr. Peltier and he immediately said, 'Well, why don't we write the biography?' and so we set about gathering the material to write what ultimately became the book *L'Étoile du Nord* [The Star of the North], published by the American College of Surgeons as a biography of Dr.

Wangensteen. I must confess that Leonard did most all of the writing. I played a role in obtaining the research for the appendices and helped a little with the writing. That effort gave us the opportunity to spend a bit of time together, and I recall one three- or four-day period when we visited the University of Minnesota gathering material to document some of the things we were writing about...[It was] an opportunity to spend not only time with Leonard, but also with Sally Wangensteen [wife of the late OHW]."[35]

Leonard F. Peltier and J. Bradley Aust, *L'Étoile du Nord: An Account of Owen Harding Wangensteen (1898-1981)* (Chicago: The American College of Surgeons, 1994).

LFP's reputation as a medical historian was further demonstrated, in addition to all his published works, by the fact that he became a resource for the New York Academy of Medicine and the National Library of Medicine, whose librarians would refer selected pertinent historical questions to him. And, he served on the editorial board of the often-cited *Familiar Medical Quotations*.[36] His legacy as a medical historian will continue to live on and be far reaching.

Notes and Sources

❧

1. Marshall R. Urist, M.D., Peltier family clipping file. Dr. Marshall Urist (1914-2001) was a distinguished orthopedic surgeon who received many awards and honors and contributed to the discipline of orthopedic surgery in a variety of ways. He taught at the University of California, Los Angeles, School of Medicine for several decades, participated in basic research, encouraged young investigators, published more than 400 articles, and edited *Clinical Orthopaedics and Related Research* from 1966 until 1993. http://dynaweb.oac.cdlib.org

2. Joseph Lister (1827-1912), a professor of surgery in London and Edinburgh and surgeon to Queen Victoria, initially introduced the concept and efficacy of antiseptic surgery in 1865. He was raised to peerage in 1897, with the title of Baron Lister. www.bartleby.com Mercer Rang, FRCS, refers to him as "Lord Lister" in his *Anthology of Orthopaedics* (New York: Churchill Livingstone, 1966), p. 2.

3. Fractures named for particular persons.

4. See History of Medicine Publications List.

5. Nancy Hulston, Archivist, Clendening History of Medicine Library and Museum, University of Kansas, personal communication to FWR, October 3, 2003.

6. Clendening History of Medicine Library and Museum. www.clendening.kumc.edu

7. Christopher Crenner, M.D., Ph.D., Interim Chair, Department of History and Philosophy of Medicine, University of Kansas School of Medicine, personal communication to FWR, September 30, 2003.

8. Logan Clendening, M.D. www.clendening.kumc.edu/lc.html

9. Ralph H. Major, M.D., *An Account of the University of Kansas School of Medicine* (Kansas City, Kansas: University of Kansas Medical Alumni Association, 1954).

10. Hannah M. Fisher, AHSC Library, letter to JGL, December 16, 1999.

11. Mary L. Riordan, AHSC Library, letter to JGL, December 28, 1999.

12. Beverly Brewster Sherrell, former Art Director, Section of Design and Illustration, Department of Learning Resources, University of Kansas Medical Center, letter to FWR, August 28, 2003.

13. Leonard F. Peltier, "John Jones: An Extraordinary American," *Surgery* 59 (1966): 631-5.

14. According to Robert P. Hudson, M.D., M.A., Professor Emeritus of the History and Philosophy of Medicine at the University of Kansas School of Medicine, the statement that John Jones published the "first American medical book"…may be true as it stands, but is arguable, as are many claims for "firsts" in medical history. Dr. Hudson explains that for the Colonial period, there is a problem of when a pamphlet becomes a monograph becomes a book. Citing Fielding Garrison's claim that the "first medical book of the Colonies appears to be" a reprint of Nicholas Culpeper's "English Physician" (1708), and John Shaw Billings' explanation that Jones' book was "the first medical book by an American author," Dr. Hudson suggests that Jones' book may more accurately be described as the "first…by an American author," rather than the "first American medical book."

15. See endnote in Plaster of Paris chapter for details about the Association of Bone and Joint Surgeons. www.abjs.org

16. Robert S. Derkash, M.D., and Richard A. Brand, M.D., "50 years of CORR," *Clinical Orthopaedics and Related Research* 414 (September 2003): 1-3.

17. Carl T. Brighton, M.D., Ph.D., Editor-in-Chief of *CORR*, letter to JGL, December 6, 1999.

18. Leonard F. Peltier, M.D., Ph.D., Classics Editor of *Clinical Orthopaedics and Related Research (CORR)*, Introduction to each of the following Classic Articles, published after his death in early May, 2003: P. S. Walker, Ching-Jen Wang, and Yann Masse, "Joint Laxity as a Criterion for the Design of Condylar Knee Prostheses," *CORR* 410 (May 2003): 5; Galen, "On the Usefulness of the Parts of the Body," *CORR* 411 (June 2003): 4; Vittorio Putti, "Historic Artificial Limbs," *CORR* 412 (July 2003): 4; and S. Weir Mitchell, "The History of Instrumental Precision in Medicine," *CORR* 413 (August 2003): 11.

19. Marshall R. Urist, M.D., Peltier family clipping file.

20. Dr. Brighton, Professor and Chair of Orthopaedic Surgery and the Paul B. Magnuson Professor of Bone and Joint Surgery at the University of Pennsylvania, was Editor-in-Chief of *CORR* from 1993 to January 2003.

21. Brighton letter to JGL, 1999.

22. Carl T. Brighton, M.D., Ph.D., letter to FWR, September 17, 2003.

23. Wilton Bunch, Guest Editor, "Ethics in Orthopaedics," Symposium in *Clinical Orthopaedics and Related Research* 378 (September 2000).

24. Gustav Flaubert, *Madam Bovary*, reprinted (New York: Penguin Books, 1950), pp. 186-98.

25. Brighton letter to FWR, 2003.

26. Maureen Finnegan, Guest Editor, "Injury Prevention," Symposium in *Clinical Orthopaedics and Related Research* 409 (April 2003).

27. Edward H. Nichols, M.D., and Frank L. Richardson, M.D., "Football Injuries of the Harvard Squad for Three Years Under the Revised Rules," *Boston Med. Surg. J.* 160 (1909): 33-7.

28. Brighton letter to FWR, 2003.

29. J. W. Dickson, "Review of Fractures: a History and Iconography of their Treatment," *Medical History* 35, 2 (April 1991): 275. www.historyofscience.com/norman_publishing

30. Laurence M. Seitz, "Review of Fractures: a History and Iconography of their Treatment," *The Journal of Orthopaedic and Sports Physical Therapy* 12, 4 (October1990): 181-2. www.historyofscience.com/norman_publishing

31. John Hall, M.D., "Fractures, History: Fractures: a History and Iconography of their Treatment," Book Review, *Journal of the American Medical Association* 264, 14 (October 10, 1990): 1879.

32. James S. Miles, M.D., "Book Review: Fractures: a History and Iconography of their Treatment," *The Journal of Bone and Joint Surgery* 72-A, 8 (September 1990): 1275.

33. Michael Bonfiglio, M.D., "Review of Orthopedics: A History and Iconography," *Journal of Bone and Joint Surgery* 75-A, 10 (October 1993): 1581-2.

34. Louis C. Almekinders, M.D., "Review of Orthopedics: A History and Iconography," *The Journal of Orthopaedic and Sports Physical Therapy* 25, 6 (June 1997): 415. www.historyofscience.com/norman_publishing

35. J. Bradley Aust, M.D., Ph.D., letter to FWR, October 5, 2003.

36. Leonard F. Peltier, Editorial Board of *Familiar Medical Quotations*, ed. Maurice B. Strauss, (Boston: Little, Brown and Company, 1968).

History of Medicine Publications

∾

Leonard F. Peltier, "A Brief Account of the Evolution of Antiseptic Surgery," *Lancet* 70 (1950): 442-4.

Leonard F. Peltier, "The Impact of Roentgen's Discovery Upon the Treatment of Fractures," *Surgery* 33 (1953): 579-86.

Leonard F. Peltier, "Eponymic Fractures: John Rhea Barton and Barton's Fracture," *Surgery* 34 (1953): 960-70.

Leonard F. Peltier, "Eponymic Fractures: Abraham Colles and Colles' Fracture," *Surgery* 35 (1954): 322-8.

Leonard F. Peltier, "Eponymic Fractures: Giovanni Battista Monteggia and Monteggia's Fracture," *Surgery* 42 (1957): 585-91.

Leonard F. Peltier, "Eponymic Fractures: Guillaume Dupuytren and Dupuytren's Fracture," *Surgery* 43 (1958): 66-74.

Leonard F. Peltier, "Eponymic Fractures: Joseph Francoise Malgaigne and Malgaigne's Fracture," *Surgery* 44 (1958): 777-84.

Leonard F. Peltier, "Eponymic Fractures: Robert William Smith and Smith's Fracture," *Surgery* 45 (1959): 1035-42.

Leonard F. Peltier, "Six Eponymic Fractures," *Bulletin of the Medical Library Association* 48 (1960): 345-51.

Leonard F. Peltier, "Bonesetting," *Surgery Gynecology and Obstetrics* 114 (1962): 252-5.

Leonard F. Peltier, "Eponymic Fractures: Percivall Pott and Pott's Fracture," *Surgery* 51 (1962): 280-6.

Leonard F. Peltier, "Introductory Biographical Note on Hugh Owen Thomas," in Hugh Owen Thomas, *Diseases of the Hip, Knee and Ankle* (a facsimile reproduction of the second edition, Boston: Little, Brown and Co., 1962).

Frederick W. Reckling and Leonard F. Peltier, "Eponymic Fractures: Riccardo Galeazzi and Galeazzi's Fracture," *Surgery* 58 (1965): 453-9.

Leonard F. Peltier, "John Jones: An Extraordinary American," *Surgery* 59 (1966): 631-5.

Leonard F. Peltier, "A History of Hip Surgery," chap. 1, in *The Adult Hip*, ed. J. J. Callaghan, Aaron Rosenberg and Harry Rubash (Lippincott-Raven Publishers, 1967).

Leonard F. Peltier, "A Brief History of Traction," *Journal of Bone and Joint Surgery* 50-A (1968): 1603-17.

Leonard F. Peltier, Editorial Board of *Familiar Medical Quotations*, ed. Maurice B. Strauss, (Boston: Little, Brown and Company, 1968).

Leonard F. Peltier, "The Role of Alessandro Codivilla in the Development of Skeletal Traction," *Journal of Bone and Joint Surgery* 51-A (1969): 1433.

Leonard F. Peltier, "The Continuity of Orthopedic Thought and Representation," *Clinical Orthopaedics and Related Research* 89 (1972): 106-11.

Leonard F. Peltier, "Eponymic Fractures: Robert Jones and Jones' Fracture," *Surgery* 71 (1972): 522-6.

Leonard F. Peltier, "John Jones: An Extraordinary American," *Bulletin of the American College of Surgeons* (March 1978): 22-5.

Leonard F. Peltier, "John Jones: An Extraordinary American," *Orthopaedic Review* 9 (1979): 19-24.

Leonard F. Peltier, "The Classic: Concerning Traumatic Malacia of the Lunate and Its Consequences: Degeneration and Compression Fractures. Privatdozent Dr. Robert Kienbock," *Clinical Orthopaedics and Related Research* 149 (1980): 4-8.

Leonard F. Peltier, "Joseph Francois Malgaigne and Malgaigne's Fracture," *Clinical Orthopaedics and Related Research* 151 (1980): 4-7.

Leonard F. Peltier, "The Classic: Concerning Arthritis Deformans Juvenilis. Professor Georg C. Perthes," *Clinical Orthopaedics and Related Research* 158 (1981): 5-9.

Leonard F. Peltier, "The Classic: Congenital Osteomalacia. Olaus Jacob Ekman," *Clinical Orthopaedics and Related Research* 159 (1981): 3-5.

Leonard F. Peltier, "The Classic: Qualities of Intellectual Order Which the Investigator Should Possess. Sant Ramon y Cajal," *Clinical Orthopaedics and Related Research* 160 (1981): 2-13.

Leonard F. Peltier, "A Brief Historical Note on the Use of Electricity in the Treatment of Fractures," *Clinical Orthopaedics and Related Research* 161 (1981): 4-7.

Leonard F. Peltier, "The Classic. Ununited Fractures in Children. James Paget, 1891," *Clinical Orthopaedics and Related Research* 166 (1982): 2-4.

Leonard F. Peltier, "The Classic. The Growth of Bone. Chapter III. Osteogenic Power of Bone Bereft of Periosteum. William Macewen, F.R.S.," *Clinical Orthopaedics and Related Research* 174 (1983): 5-14.

Leonard F. Peltier, "The 'Back School' of Delpech in Montpellier," *Clinical Orthopaedics and Related Research* 179 (1983): 4-9.

Leonard F. Peltier, "Guerin versus Malgaigne: A Precedent for the Free Criticism of Scientific Papers," *Journal of Orthopaedic Research* 1 (1983): 115-8.

Leonard F. Peltier, "Fractures of the Distal End of the Radius: An Historical Account," *Clinical Orthopaedics and Related Research* 187 (1984): 18-22.

Leonard F. Peltier, "Joseph Guichard Duverney (1648-1730): Champion of Applied Comparative Anatomy," *Clinical Orthopaedics and Related Research* 187 (1984): 308-11.

Leonard F. Peltier, "The Classic. Separations of the Epiphyses. By Jean Timothee Emile Foucher. 1867," *Clinical Orthopaedics and Related Research* 188 (1984): 3-9.

Leonard F. Peltier, "Geronimo Mecuriali (1530-1606) and the First Illustrated Book on Sports Medicine," *Clinical Orthopaedics and Related Research* 198 (1985): 21-4.

Leonard F. Peltier, "Historical Note on Bone and Soft Tissue Sarcoma," *Journal of Surgical Oncology* 30 (1985): 201-5.

Leonard F. Peltier, "Nicolas Andry: The Designer of Orthopedic Iconography," *Clinical Orthopaedics and Related Research* 200 (1985): 54-6.

Leonard F. Peltier, "The Division of Orthopaedic Surgery in the A.E.F., a.k.a. The Goldthwait Unit," *Clinical Orthopaedics and Related Research* 200 (1985): 45-9.

Leonard F. Peltier, "The Orthopedist Who Invented the Chain Saw" (Bernhard Heine), *Bulletin of the American Academy of Orthopaedic Surgeons* (May 1985): 31.

Leonard F. Peltier, "The Case of the Limping Victim" (Guillaume Dupuytren), *Bulletin of the American Academy of Orthopaedic Surgeons* (December 1985): 17.

Leonard F. Peltier, "A Day in the Life of a Resident" (George W. Bagby), *Bulletin of the American Academy of Orthopaedic Surgeons* (January 1986): 21.

Leonard F. Peltier, "Volkmann: Surgeon, Poet, Storyteller," *Bulletin of the American Academy of Orthopaedic Surgeons* (July 1986): 25.

Leonard F. Peltier, "Wattmann: a Pioneer of Orthopaedic Manikins," *Bulletin of the American Academy of Orthopaedic Surgeons* (October 1986): 30.

Leonard F. Peltier, "The Lineage of Sports Medicine," *Clinical Orthopaedics and Related Research* 216 (1987): 4-12.

Leonard F. Peltier, "The Case of The Subcutaneous Achilles Tenotomy" (Gustav Flaubert), *Bulletin of the American Academy of Orthopaedic Surgeons* (January 1987): 16.

Leonard F. Peltier, "A Case of an Ununited Fracture of the Humerus Cured by the Use of a Seton" (Philip Syng Physick), *Bulletin of the American Academy of Orthopaedic Surgeons* (April 1987): 23.

Leonard F. Peltier, "Indications for Hip Arthroplasty" (John Rhea Barton), *Bulletin of the American Academy of Orthopaedic Surgeons* (July 1987): 33.

Leonard F. Peltier, "Cross Section Anatomy Revisited" (Nikolai Ivanovich Pirogoff), *Bulletin of the American Academy of Orthopaedic Surgeons* (January 1988): 27.

Leonard F. Peltier, M.D., and John H. Davis, M.D., "A History of the American Association for the Surgery of Trauma: The First 50 Years," *The Journal of Trauma* 29, 2 (1989): 143-151.

Leonard F. Peltier, *Fractures: A History and Iconography of Their Treatment* (San Francisco: Norman Publishing, 1990).

Leonard F. Peltier, "Historical Perspective," chap. 1 in Frederick W. Reckling, JoAnn B. Reckling and Melvin P. Mohn, *Orthopaedic Anatomy and Surgical Approaches* (St. Louis: Mosby Year Book, 1990), 3-5.

Leonard F. Peltier, "Introduction (a biography of Hugh Owen Thomas)," in Hugh Owen Thomas, *Diseases of the Hip, Knee and Ankle Joints* (San Francisco: Norman Publishing, 1991).

Leonard F. Peltier, *Orthopedics: A History and Iconography* (San Francisco: Norman Publishing, 1993).

Leonard F. Peltier and J. Bradley Aust, *L'Étoile du Nord: An Account of Owen Harding Wangensteen (1898-1981)* (Chicago: The American College of Surgeons, 1994).

Leonard F. Peltier and Nguyen Thi Nga, "Useful Hints for the Study of the History of Orthopaedics," *Clinical Orthopaedics and Related Research* 309 (1994): 267-73.

Leonard F. Peltier, "Cabeza de Vaca: The First European to Practice Medicine in North America Travels Through Arizona," *The Sombrero* (90th Anniversary Issue) (October 1994).

Leonard F. Peltier, "The Patron Saints of Medicine," *Clinical Orthopaedics and Related Research* 334 (1997): 374-9.

Leonard F. Peltier, "A Classic in Trauma Education," *Clinical Orthopaedics and Related Research* 339 (1997): 4-6.

Leonard F. Peltier, "A Case of Extraordinary Exostoses on the Back of a Boy. 1740. John Freke (1688-1756)," *Clinical Orthopaedics and Related Research* 346 (1998): 5-6.

T. B. Hunter, L. F. Peltier, and P. J. Lund, "Radiologic History Exhibit. Musculoskeletal Eponyms: Who Are Those Guys?" *Radiographics* 20, 3 (2000): 819-36.

Leonard F. Peltier, Editor, "Symposium on the History of Orthopedics in North America," *Clinical Orthopaedics and Related Research* 374 (2000).

Leonard F. Peltier, "Geometric Total Knee Replacement: Operative Considerations, Lee Hunter Riley, Jr., M.D., 1973," *Clinical Orthopaedics and Related Research* 380 (2000): 3-8.

CHAPTER TEN

The Later Years

"Dear Len,

If it is true that you are turning 80, then there is something wrong with you. Your general behavior, the way you talk, your plans in the carving territory, are telling me that you are the same orthopedic cowboy I have known for a good 20 years."

— MILOS CHVAPIL, M.D., PH.D.[1]
PROFESSOR AND HEAD, RETIRED
SECTION OF SURGICAL BIOLOGY
UNIVERSITY OF ARIZONA COLLEGE OF MEDICINE

When Marian Peltier first visited Tucson in 1970, she exclaimed, "Leonard, I think we have just landed on the moon!"[2] In spite of this first impression, the Peltiers quickly embraced their new community and became "Westerners." After a short time on the job in Tucson, LFP often abandoned his more conventional mid-western attire for cowboy boots, bolo string ties and a cowboy hat with a solid Indian-silver hatband. Marian and Leonard, long-time gourmet cooks, took up preparing southwest cuisine with a passion. They traveled to Alamos, Mexico, to attend cooking classes. LFP began to refer to the Peltier residence in Tucson as "Huesos Viejos (old bones) Ranch" and placed the name on his personal letterhead.

He contacted Phoenix to inquire about getting a brand for his "ranch." This proved unsuccessful due to government regulations, but many years later in 1986, two of his graduating residents (Keith Braun, M.D., and Michael Parseghian, M.D.) had a branding iron welded with the HV logo. The "branding iron" adorned LFP's library wall for many years.

LFP acquired a horse and took up horseback riding for exercise, relaxation and recreation. During these undertakings, shared with friends and colleagues, many topics were discussed. One fellow horseman,[3] in a letter directed to LFP, related: "I have in my memory our horseback riding adventures, meeting the joggers with a friendly suggestion 'get a horse.' Another time when we were in the operatic mode, you were singing with a strong and melodic voice some arias from your beloved Wagner's Tristan and Isolde, and I tried, with much inferior voice, some Dvorak and Smetana heroes. I learned from you

LFP on Horseback

Photo courtesy of James Benjamin

HUESOS VIEJOS RANCH
L. F. Peltier, Prop.
5251 N. Via Condesa
Tucson, Arizona 85718

many facts and gossips about several composers. Do you remember how you talked about papa Brahms babysitting for Schumann's children (and you knew that they were seven) and his love for Clara [Schumann]?[4] In spite of my great interest in music and the life of musicians, you were always ahead of my actual knowledge.

"Equally interesting for me were our professional discussions, where your analysis of many of my problems, confusions, were with great insight answered due to your great knowledge of pathophysiology. These discussions took place on horseback as well as in my office…or on our way to various restaurants. Anytime you walked into my office you had either the [solution] to some of my problems, or vice versa, you came asking my view of some of your professional problems. And how I liked your giving me a preview on your books, the history of cripples, stories about 'surgery' in various centuries, etc.

"How relaxing and enjoyable were our dinners. Marian and Milena understood each other very well and each of us tried to surprise the other couple with discovering a new, exciting restaurant with some specials."[5]

While appreciating a multitude of new experiences offered by their Tucson surroundings, Marian and LFP placed family relationships high on their personal priority list. During their first winter in Arizona, LFP flew to Wisconsin Rapids to bring his widowed father George to live with them in Tucson. LFP's father was in his mid-eighties with progressing visual difficulties due to macular degeneration. At that time he could only perceive light and dark. When his health deteriorated further, he was relocated to an assisted-living center and died in Tucson in 1975 at age eighty-seven.

LFP stopped operating on patients during the early 1980s. This was a difficult decision but he "didn't want to continue operating past his prime." He continued to see patients and carry out his teaching and administrative responsibilities as Chief of the Section of Orthopedic Surgery at the University of Arizona (UA). When LFP saw patients in his clinic who needed surgical intervention, he referred them to an appropriate associate at UA, based on the area of required expertise.

LFP retired as chief of the orthopedic section at UA in 1985 when he was sixty-five years old, intending to continue as a faculty member in the section, but not as an administrator. However, approximately a year later he accepted an appointment as Acting Head of the Department of Surgery at UA and served in this capacity until July 1990, at which time a permanent department chair was appointed. This later stint as acting surgery chair was especially difficult, according to Carolyn Kelsey,[6] his administrative assistant during the two occasions he served in this position. The department and the faculty were larger the second time (1986-90), and health maintenance organizations (HMOs) had made a huge impact on the department. Dr. Peltier was older and his health status was changing. His chronic asthma persisted. He noticed the incipient onset of decreased visual acuity and was found to have macular degeneration. He developed thrombophlebitis in his leg, a blood clot and a subsequent pulmonary embolus, which required hospitalization.

Because of long-standing degenerative arthritis that began in his late forties, LFP underwent total knee surgery during this time period. His successful bilateral unicompartmental knee replacements allowed him to personally benefit from the remarkable technological advances in orthopedic surgery and the section he had built at UA. The operations were performed on the same day (thus under one anesthetic), in his own bailiwick (University of Arizona Hospital) and by one of his associates (Dr. Robert Volz). The knee replacements served him well for the rest of his days.

When LFP truly retired from UA in 1990, the surgery department honored him with a large retirement celebration May 4 at the La Paloma Resort in Tucson. At this time the establishment of the Leonard F. Peltier Research award for surgical residents at UA was announced. "The Leonard F. Peltier Chairman's award, supported by funds donated by him and deposited in the University of Arizona Foundation, was established to recognize research, both clinical and basic, by surgery residents. It [was] open to all residents in the Department of Surgery [including orthopedic residents, as orthopedics was not a separate department at that time]. Three prizes are awarded at a Resident Research Symposium, usually in May or June. Several recipients of these research awards have gone on to very successful academic careers."[7]

During his retirement, LFP pursued his love for the history of medicine despite his gradual, but progressive, visual difficulties. A library associate describes how he continued his work and simultaneously dealt with his visual problems: "When personal computers appeared on the scene, he became entranced with them. He learned many different computing programs, and was an adept user of the library online catalogue and an avid e-mail user. In addition to being fluent in French and German, he also possessed a working knowledge of Italian, Spanish and other languages. The fact that a published article might not be in

English was never a formidable obstacle for Dr. Peltier. The library staff often received messages from him. His e-mail messages to the library usually started out: 'I'm looking for...'

"As his visual impairment gradually increased, he purchased and taught himself to use 'zoom' text software and a scanner that enabled him to enlarge the information displayed on his computer screen. He was not at all deterred and continued to read and write in spite of these problems. At one of our coffee breaks he mentioned that his father also had visual problems and had devised methods to compensate for the impairment. Realizing that his vision was becoming a potential hazard, Dr. Peltier relinquished his driver's license and Mrs. Peltier became the 'chauffeur.' He jokingly said that he would never be critical about Mrs. Peltier's driving again, 'lest I become a walker.'

"Dr. Peltier could speak eloquently on any number of medical topics, yet he also could sit and talk passionately about art, the humanities, politics, and music, and his excitement over the latest sporting events. For more than twenty years, Dr. Peltier and I rooted for our favorite teams in the NCAA, NBA and Super Bowl championship games. We seldom agreed and naturally we bet on who would be the winner. Our wagers were for a 35-cent cup of coffee in the hospital cafeteria. Dr. Peltier was both a gracious winner and loser. He would say. 'Until next year...'and 'they are both great teams.'"[8]

In addition to pursuing historical interests via the library, LFP took advantage of opportunities to explore a variety of places. In 1993 Marian and LFP celebrated their fiftieth wedding anniversary with a cruise through the Panama Canal. In 1996 they enjoyed a month-long cruise that started in the Pacific, included the Galapagos Islands, continued around Cape Horn at the southern tip of South America, and ended in Miami. Their last such excursion was a Baltic Sea Cruise in 1999, with their son George and his wife Claudia, that took them to many ports, including St. Petersburg, Russia.

In 1997 Marian and Leonard moved to Albuquerque, New Mexico, to be near their son Steve and his family. LFP remarked that as they aged and his vision declined, their sons had delivered an ultimatum: "you *do* have a choice: you may move to either Albuquerque or

Minneapolis." Given the climate differences between the two cities, LFP said that decision "took them about five seconds." Although they were both in their late seventies, they bought a new home and embraced their new situation with vigor and a positive outlook. They explored their new surroundings, riding the Toltec and Cumbres railroad out of Chama, NM, with Steve and his family, enjoyed visits from George and his family, and entertained friends from Tucson. According to LFP, "One of our main pleasures now is following the careers of our grandchildren… fortunately there will be a quorum of family in Albuquerque for Christmas…we are very happy living [here] and have found it…interesting…." After LFP's death, Steve's wife, Lanie, commented how wonderful it had been to have them geographically nearby for the past few years. The frequent face-to-face contact and LFP's vast knowledge and droll sense of humor enriched their busy lives!

LFP, an undisputed polymath,[9] was forever learning and taking on new projects. One of his former residents described him as "a pedantic skeptic grounded in a pragmatic, common sense philosophy, made powerful by native intelligence and deeply-rooted education."[10] When he began horseback riding, not only did he learn to ride, but he learned to care for the animals. He studied wood-carving at the local

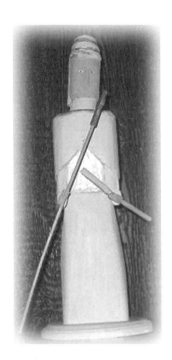

Pope Gregory the Great
One of the Patron Saints of Music

Gregory is shown with the triple crown of the papacy, carrying his crozier (a staff similar to a shepherd's crook carried as a symbol of office) in one hand and a sheaf of music in the other. In LFP's words, accompanying the gift, "I like the brighter lighter colors better than the dull darker colors usually seen in many of the little carvings of the saints."

Photo courtesy of Janolyn Lo Vecchio

According to Milos Chvapil, recipient of these gifts, "The one with horns [on the left] is Hundig the brute, a character from Richard Wagner's opera Die Walkure; the middle one is a Mexican patron saint of cripples, and the painted face on the log is a spirit, given to us to protect us and our new mountain cabin."

Photo courtesy of Milos Chvapil

community colleges in Tucson and Albuquerque, and after his retirement, he began carving "santos," primitive art images of saints. He gave a number of these carvings to special friends, explaining their origin and meaning. Typically, he learned as much as he could about the saints he was carving, and in 1997 he published an article entitled "The Patron Saints of Medicine."[11]

LFP's years as a program chief, teaching medical students and residents,

Moses
∾
*Photo courtesy of
Federico Adler*

have not been forgotten. In 1994 the Peltier-trained former orthopedic residents from the Universities of Kansas and Arizona donated $85,000 to the Section of Orthopedic Surgery at the University of Kansas to establish an annual Peltier Lectureship to commemorate Dr. Peltier's leadership. The Lectureship's inaugural speaker, by invitation, in the spring of 1994 was LFP himself, who presented a biographical account of Owen H. Wangensteen in the Clendening History of Medicine amphitheater on the campus of the University of Kansas Medical Center. The talk, entitled "Owen H. Wangensteen: Surgeon, Teacher, Scholar," was excerpted from his and Dr. Brad Aust's nearly completed book,

The Leonard F. Peltier, M.D., Ph.D.
Orthopedic Lectureship
University of Kansas
∾

"Owen H. Wangensteen: Surgeon, Teacher, Scholar"
Leonard F. Peltier, April 29, 1994

"Quest for the Artificial Joint"
Frederick W. Reckling, M.D., June 2, 1995

"History of the Surgical Treatment of Scoliosis"
John E. Hall, M.D., June 7, 1996

"History of Charnley the Man"
John J. Callaghan, M.D., August 1, 1997

"Osteolysis and Aseptic Loosening"
Harry Rubash, M.D., November 19, 1998

"Women and the Orthopedic Surgeon:
Changing the Relationship"
Laura Tosi, M.D., July 28, 2000

"Molecular and Genetic Applications to Spine Surgery"
James D. Kang, M.D., April 12, 2002

LFP delivering first Leonard F. Peltier lecture in Clendening
Amphitheater

∾

"Owen H. Wangensteen: Surgeon, Teacher, Scholar"

Photo courtesy of Federico Adler

L'Étoile du Nord.[12] At the time of the lecture, they had not yet arrived at a name for the biography, but shortly thereafter decided that OHW was, indeed, "the star of the north."

First Peltier Lectureship Banquet
Federico Adler (KU '60), LFP, Bob Orr (KU '59)

Bob Orr was the first resident accepted into the residency program (1957)
by LFP as new orthopedics chairman at Kansas.

Photo courtesy of Federico Adler

This event was followed by a black-tie banquet at the Alameda Plaza hotel on Kansas City's unique Country Club Plaza, honoring Dr. Peltier and his immediate family. Marian's contributions to LFP's career were recognized as well, and roses were presented to her by their sons. The celebration's afternoon and evening programs were well attended by general surgeons as well as orthopedists from the Kansas City area. The lectureship continues to be a regular event with various pertinent scholarly topics presented by invited speakers.

As LFP approached his eightieth birthday, in the year 2000, Janolyn Lo Vecchio continued to pursue her goal of writing a biography of LFP as a birthday gift for him. She solicited and received letters or phone calls from nearly fifty friends and colleagues across the nation. Previously she had completed a series of interviews with him, when, in 1996-7, Marian would drive him to AHSC for the weekly orthopedic X-ray conferences. After the conference, he would visit his friends in the medical library for research and social purposes, as well as meet with Ms. Lo Vecchio. Those interviews, along with the collection of letters and a very complete, updated curriculum vitae, formed the core of this biography. As Ms. Lo Vecchio was completing her first draft and clarifying some information, LFP inquired, "You seem to have amassed quite a bit of material. Am I going to be permitted to review it?" In typical fashion, he edited, commented, clarified, and added material, but emphasized in a follow-up letter that the content is "all yours." He further remarked, "For me the most important part is the letters. It is not often that a man gets to hear things that are usually said at his funeral. Most people have a good idea of who they are, but very few, or none, ever see or understand how people perceive their persona. Many of the incidents that seemed so important to the residents and staff, I do not even remember as being significant at the time. Thank you so much for soliciting the letters. They are very important to me."[13]

In the early spring of 2003 LFP was seen at the Mayo Clinic because of general malaise and unexplained anemia. He was found to have a kidney carcinoma (cancer) that was successfully removed, but two days later, after an uneventful initial recovery from the operation, he experienced a cardio-respiratory arrest and died unexpectedly in Rochester, Minnesota on 4 May 2003. He was eighty-three at the time.

At his memorial service in Albuquerque on 10 May 2003, his accomplishments, wit, generosity, and acts of kindness were recalled by family members, friends and colleagues who traveled from Europe and across the United States. During the events of that sad and memorable weekend, Ms. Lo Vecchio approached FWR and JBR for assistance in getting this biography published. Welcoming the opportunity to add further dimensions to the book, particularly those of a fellow orthopedist, academic program chairman, faculty nurse, and academic wife, as well as collecting pertinent additional information, the challenge was readily accepted. We only wish LFP could have had the opportunity to review this final effort!

Additionally, an endowed Professorship and Chair of Orthopedic Surgery (the Peltier/Reckling Alumni Professor and Chair of Orthopedic Surgery) is in developmental stages at the University of Kansas Hospital and School of Medicine. Unfortunately, although plans for the endowed professorship and chair were underway when LFP became ill, he was not aware of this important honor.

We will miss you Leonard! *Onward and upward!*

Leonard F. Peltier, M.D., Ph.D.
1997

∾

Photo courtesy of the Peltier family

Notes and Sources

ॐ

1. Milos Chvapil, M.D., Ph.D., letter to JGL, December 28, 1999.

2. Robert G. Volz, M.D., personal communication to FWR, October 2003.

3. Chvapil letter, 1999.

4. "Schumann's death in 1856, after years of agonizing mental illness, deeply affected Brahms. He remained a devoted friend of Schumann's family; his correspondence with Schumann's widow Clara reveals a deep affection and spiritual intimacy, but the speculation about their friendship growing into a romance exists only in the fevered imaginations of psychologizing biographers." Nicolas Slonimsky, *The Concise Baker's Biographical Dictionary of Musicians* (New York: Schirmer Books, Macmillan, Inc., 1988), p. 161.

5. Chvapil letter, 1999.

6. Carolyn Kelsey, Executive Assistant, Department of Surgery, interview by JGL, March 19, 1999.

7. Dr. Charles Putnam, e-mail communication to JGL, March 30, 2000.

8. Nga Nguyen, Information Services, Arizona Health Sciences Library, letter to FWR, August 5, 2003.

9. polymath: a person of great and varied learning

10. James Glenn, M.D. (KU '73), written communication with JGL, Fall 1999.

11. Leonard F. Peltier, "The Patron Saints of Medicine," *Clinical Orthopaedics and Related Research* 334 (1997): 374-9.

12. Leonard F. Peltier and J. Bradley Aust, *L'Étoile du Nord: An Account of Owen Harding Wangensteen (1898-1981)* (Chicago: The American College of Surgeons, 1994).

13. Leonard F. Peltier, letter to JGL, March 13, 2000. *(Authors' note: the letters have not been reprinted in their entirety, but many excerpts have been included throughout the text).*

Index

∽

(Authors' note: page numbers in bold italics refer to illustrations and their legends and credits)

∽A

~H

Hagan, Cary, xxii, 150
Hague, The, 41
handshake, 82
hand surgery, xii, 71, 85
Hanlon, C. Rollins, xx
Harrington, Paul, 155
Harvard University, v, 31, 155, 161, *161*, 168
Harvill, Richard A., 61 – 2
head trauma, 127
Heap, Ralph, xix, *71*, *96 – 7*
heart surgeon, 69
heel, 87
Heidenreich, Fred L., xx, 78
helicopter, viii, 106, 108
Hennepin County Medical Center, 15, *92*
Henry Ford Hospital, 83
Hermreck, Arlo, xxii, 103, 123
high school, vi, 2 – 3, 5 – 6, 60, *92*
Hippolyte, 160
Hip Society, xiii, 78
history(-ian, -ical) (see also *Clinical Orthopaedics and Related Research; Fractures; L'Étoile; Orthopedics*, University of Kansas, Clendening History of Medicine Library and Museum)
   Arizona, xv, xxi, 59 – 63, 76, 120
   Friesen, 11, 31, 35, 55
   Hudson, xxi, 55
   Kansas, xxii, 35 – 8, 40, 45, 48, 51, 154 – 7, 180
   LFP, xiii – vii, xxv, 43, 48, 53, 73, 88, 110 – 1, *115*, 153 – 72, 175 – 7, 180
   Major, 57, 154, 157
   medical education, 12 – 3, 56, 76 – 7
   medical history, 55, 63, 88, 110 – 1, *115*, 121, 149, 153 – 72, 180
   military, 32
   Minnesota, xxi, 11 – 5
   patient, 88
   Wangensteen, 9, 153

Hitchcock
   Claude, 22
   Claudia, *92*
Hixon Hall (see University of Kansas)
Hoenecke, Heinz, *71 – 2*
Holderman, Wallace D., xix, 38, *42*, *96 – 7*
holiday, iv, 28, 30, 95
Holy Ghost, 69
home study program, 112
honesty (see also ethics), 82, 84, 86
horse, v, 87, 174, *174*, 178
House of Lords, 112
Howorth, Beckett, xvii
Hoyt, Walter A., 64
Hudson, Robert P., xxi – ii, 55 – 7, *119*, 167
Huesos Viejos, 173, *174*
Hulston, Nancy, xxii, 166
humor, xvi, xxi, 5, 43 – 4, 46, 53, *69*, 73, 160, 178
Hundig the brute, *179*
hydroxyapatite, 146
hypoxia, 130 – 1, 133

~I

Infantile Paralysis, National Foundation for, 24, 26
infantry, 7, 16
in-patient, xii
instrument(s)
   musical, 6, *116*
   scientific, 24
   surgical, 50, 70, 87, 89, *116*, 154, 163, 167
instrumentation, 70, 77, 88, 155
integrity (see also ethics), 82, 84, 87
international, xxv, 47, 50 – 1, 65 – 6, 70 – 1, 120 – 1
internship
   LFP, 18 – 9
   other, 14, 18, 78, 83 – 4, 102

∾M

~*T*

❧

About the Author

Janolyn Lo Vecchio worked in the orthopedic surgery section at the University of Arizona College of Medicine from 1975-85, and was Dr. Peltier's administrative assistant for six years. With his encouragement, she began attending college part-time while working full time, and graduated with a B.S. in Education from the University of Arizona in 1986.

Since retiring from the University of Arizona, College of Medicine in 1996, Janolyn is a speaker and writer on Arizona women's history. Her latest book, *Women Who Made A Difference*, was published in September 2003. She is the recipient of the James Elliott Award for historical writing from the Arizona Historical Society.

Janolyn Lo Vecchio

About the Authors

JoAnn and Fred Reckling

ᴥ

*F*rederick W. Reckling, M.D., Professor Emeritus, Department of Orthopedic Surgery, University of Kansas School of Medicine, knew Leonard Peltier as a training chief, co-faculty member, fellow chair of an academic program, and most importantly as a friend, mentor, and role model for more than forty years. JoAnn B. Reckling, RN, Ph.D., first met Leonard in her capacity as a young staff nurse, caring for orthopedic patients at the University of Kansas Medical Center. Leonard and Marian Peltier served as professional and academic faculty family role models for her as she pursued her professional goals, teaching nursing at KU, obtaining graduate degrees in nursing with philosophy and ethics majors, publishing, and maintaining her family responsibilities as an academic chairman's wife and mother of two children.

Fred and JoAnn have retired in Fort Collins, Colorado, near Fred's native Wyoming, and continue to pursue their interests in writing and family, enjoying their children and their families, including four grandchildren.

ᴥ